THE BANJARA

CASTES AND TRIBES OF INDIA-SERIES

1. Continuity and Change Among the Ahom/ **Nitul Kumar Gogai**
2. Ethnography of a Nomadic Tribe: A Study of Yanadi/ **N. Sudhakar Rao**
3. Mythos and Logos of the Warlis: A Tribal World View/ **Ajay Dandekar (Ed)**
4. Naga Cultural Attires and Musical Instruments/ **A. Lanu Ao (Ed.)**
5. Socio-Cultural Study of Scheduled Tribes: The Pardhans of Maharashtra/ **S.R. Murkute**
6. The Banjara/ **S.G. Deogaonkar** and **Shailaja S. Deogaonkar**
7. The Kolam Tribals/ **S.G. Deogaonkar** and **Leena Deogaonkar Baxi**
8. The Korku Tribals/ **S.G. Deogaonkar** and **Shailaja S. Deogaonkar**
9. Tribal Dance and Songs/ **S.G. Deogaonkar** and **Shailaja S. Deogaonkar**

About the Authors

DR. S.G. DEOGAONKAR is a scholar of repute and his field of specialisation is Political and Social Anthropology, Tribal Development and Constitutional Law. He has participated in numerous conferences and seminars including the Xth International Congress of Anthropological and Ethnological Science. He was a Member on the District Planning and Development Council of the Chandrapur district and Chancellor's Nominee on the Nagpur University Senate. Dr. Deogaonkar was a Member-Participant of the Socio-Economic Groups on Scheduled Castes and Scheduled Tribes for formulation of the Eighth Five Year Plan Schemes constituted under the Backward Classes Division of the Planning Commission. He has completed many post-doctoral research projects for the UGC and ICSSR and was a National (Post-doctoral) Research Fellow in Tribal Development of the Ministry of Welfare, Government of India. He has published numerous works like *Administration of Rural Development in India*; *The Hill Korwa*; *The Korku Tribals*; *The Madia of Bhamragad*; *Tribal Development Through Tribal Sub-plan*; *Political Anthropology*; *Tribal Exploitation*, etc.

At present, Dr. Deogaonkar is working as Head, Department of Political Science at the Anand Niketan College, Warora (Maharashtra.)

DR. (MRS.) SHAILAJA S. DEOGAONKAR holds a Masters Degree in Marathi Literature and a Ph. D. in Tribal Linguistics. She has completed post-doctoral research project for the ICSSR and has done documentation of tribal dialect and folk-lore for the Maharashta branch of the Indian National Theatre. Mrs. Deogaonkar has collected and analyzed the tribal genre for the prominent tribes from Vidarbha and has written quite a number of books and contributed papers at many Seminars and Conferences as well as published articles in academic journals.

Castes and Tribes of India-3

THE BANJARA

S.G. DEOGAONKAR

SHAILAJA S. DEOGAONKAR

CONCEPT PUBLISHING COMPANY PVT. LTD.
NEW DELHI-110059

ISBN: 978-81-7022-433-4

First Published 1992

Published and Printed by

Concept Since 1974

Concept Publishing Company Pvt. Ltd.
A/15-16, Commercial Block, Mohan Garden,
New Delhi-110059 (India)
T: 91-11-41101460
E: publishing@conceptpub.com, *W*: www.conceptpub.com

PREFACE

THE BANJARA Community is one of the most colourful, attractive and interesting group not only for the common man but also for anthropologist. The group has been classified as a *nomadic tribe* and is found in Gujarat, Madhya Pradesh, Maharashtra, Karnataka and parts of Andhra Pradesh and Orissa. Earlier, people were terrified when a Banjara *Tanda* come near a town, due to the rumours that they kidnap children and also that they indulge in criminal activities or robberies. The real life and activities of this community remained obscure. While on one hand they were looked down upon as a backward and dangerous tribe, they claimed themselves to be of great loyalty and integrity tracing their ethnic descent from the Rajputs of Mewad.

It is difficult to compromise with the word 'tribe' when one studies the Banjara community. The level of acculturation is so different from other tribes in India that the usual criteria applied for designating any group the status of a tribe hardly apply to them. The real status was nomadism which came due to their occupation and their practice of moving out with families. Hence the settled Banjaras in Vidarbha region of Maharashtra show a fully acculturised social life with socialisation almost similar to the non-tribal people in the area. Their is a strong Hindu culture with an intermixing of Sikhism in some cases. State and National level leaders have come-up from this community in Vidarbha area. Their folk-literature is also rich and reflects and non-material values.

We found it rewarding to study this nomadic tribe and are glad to present this monograph on the community. We were assisted in our field investigations by student and non-student youths from the Banjara Community.

Many other Banjara friends from different areas made available valuable material, folk-literature etc. We are extremely thankful to all of them. Our thanks are also due to the Concept Publishing Company for publishing this work.

We hope, this book will be well received by scholars and common readers as well.

Warora

S.G. DEOGAONKAR
SHAILAJA S. DEOGAONKAR

CONTENTS

CHAPTER I

THE BANJARAS
Their Habitat and Identification

THE BANJARA community which is classified as a Nomodic tribe is one of the most colourful and progressive group which displays a level of acculturation rarely found in any other groups from the backward communities. It has a long history of migration, of occupation, and, a present which shows rapid progress. The homeland of the Banjaras in Vidarbha area of Maharashtra is the Yeotmal district and the community has settled there fanning out in the adjoining districts of Vidarbha and Marathwada regions of Maharashtra. This community has the proud privilege of providing two Chief Ministers of Maharashtra and atleast two Cabinet Ministers in the Maharashtra Cabinet.

It was very interesting to study this community which stands distinct against the back-drop of many tribal groups in this region.

Habitat

Traditionally, their main habitat was described in Central Provinces and Berar, and in Hyderabad i.e. the erstwhile Nizam State. Similarly, they were also found in the erstwhile Bombay State. According to 1911 census 56,000 persons from Central Provinces, 80,000 in Berar and 174,000 from Hyderabad were reported. Thus, their main habitat was the Deccan plateau. Presently, these areas include Vidarbha region, some parts of Maharashtra, Andhra Pradesh and Madhya Pradesh. Sizeable concentration of the Banjara is found in the Yeotmal district and adjoining part of Amravati district, parts of Akola district in Vidarbha, Nanded district from Marathwada in Maharashtra, Named district of Madhya Pradesh and the areas around Hyderabad in Andhra Pradesh. They are also found in lesser concentration in the Parbhani, Dhulia and Jalgaon districts of Maharashtra (Khandesh) and also in parts of Karnataka, Uttar

Pradesh, and Gujarat and in their home i.e., Rajasthan.

Some Banjaras have also been spotted in Orissa.

The Banjara population in Vidarbha is mainly concentrated in the Yeotmal district particularly in Pusad, Pandharkawada, Digras areas, maximum being in Pusad tehsil.

They have also spread to Amravati and Akola districts and very few to the Chandrapur district and Buldhana districts. The Banjaras are also found in Nanded, Hingoli, Parbhani and Mahur areas. In Khandesh area, they are found in Jalgaon, Dhulia and Chalisgaon.

It is an important to note that the Banjara in Vidarbha, and that too from the Yeotmal district, are the most settled community with a lot of Socio-economic change in occupational structure and development. They have been assimilated in the main stream of Socio-Political current of Vidarbha as well as of Maharashtra, and still maintain many colourful as well as traditional aspects of culture. They have provided leadership to the area and to the Maharashtra State which was accepted by local/regional people. Hence, the Banjara from Vidarbha deserve special place in the process of acculturation/socialization of this nomadic tribe.

Nomenclature

As per the etymology given by different scholars the word Banjara has its roots in :

Van-jārā – The inhabitants or the burners of forest.
OR
Biranjār – (A Persian word) Meaning rice carriers. (Quoted from Shakespeare's Dictionary)
Banjārā – An arrow.
Vana-Charā – (Sanskrit) a wanderer in Jungle.
Labhān (From lavan) – Carriers of Salt (A sub-division of Banjara)

Another interpretation also corroborates some of the roots stated above and puts forth the following.

Van + Ja + ari (Sanskrit) Meaning foes of the forest or in the forest because they used to loot people passing through forest or destroy forest.

Vanijyā in Sanskrit is *Banaj* in Hindi – hence those who indulged in Banaj-trading could be Banjārā. In Urdu, *Banjar* means fallow land (in Marathi-*Banjad*), and those who lived on it could be called Banjara.[1]

Different names are used to describe this community. Russell and Hiralal, quoting Cumberlege have mentioned Banjara, Wanjari, Labhana and Mukeri as the alternatives for the same community. In 1965, the Government of Maharashtra specified the following, as castes/groups within Banjara.

> (1) Gor-Banjara (2) Lambhada, Labhana (3) Charan Banjara. (4) Laman, (5) Mathura-Labhan, (6) Kachakivale Banjara, (7) Lamana Banjara, (8) Laman-Lamani, (9) Labhan, (10) Nahavi Banjara, (11) Jogi Banjara, (12) Shingada Banjara, (13) Dhadi, (14) Dhalida, (15) Shingavale Banjari.

In July 1983 the Government of Maharashtra again notified certain Backward castes/groups for the purposes of reservation. Under Banjara, were also included :

Banjara, Banjari, Vanjara, Mathura-Banjara, Gor-Banjara, Lambada/Lambara, Lambhani, Charan Banjara, Labhan, Mathura-Labhani, Kachkiwala Banjara, Laman Banjara, Laman-Lamani, Laban, Ghali/Dhalia, Dhadi/Ghadi, Singri, Navi Banjara, Jogi-Banjara, Shingade-Banjara, Lambade, Phanade Banjara, Sunar Banjara, Dhalya Banjara, Shingadiya Banjara.

Migration of the Community

The habitat under study is not the original habitat of this nomadic-tribe. It is a group which hails originally from Rajasthan or Rajputana. Todd refers to their migration from Rajputana between 1784 to 1818 and when they were recognised as Banjaras. The king of Mewad issued a manifesto in 1855 in which he refers to the Banjara as a nomadic and trading group. It is stated that they accompanied the Mughal army as supplier of food-grains and they had taken contract from the Mughal king for this purpose. There are references of the Banjara supplying food-grains even to the Marathas, while on expeditions. Gen. Briggs refers to them as suppliers of food-grains to the Nizam and English army in 1798, but they were dispersed after Tipu's death in 1799. The English rulers also bestowed bounties upon them. It is due to this historical fact that references to Banjaras appear in a Mysore Government publication of 1901 based on the census report of 1901, Berar Gazetteer, and the Linguistic survey of Indian by Prof. Grierson.

The Banjaras from the Pusad area of Yeotmal district believe that they migrated from Rajasthan 300 to 500 years ago, after the war between Prithviraj Chauvan and the Mughal emperor. The main reason for their migration was the continuous battles between the Muhamadens and Hindu rulers. According to some returns, they migrated from Mewad/Marwad to Maharashtra, Andhra Pradesh Karnataka, Gujarat, Madhya Pradesh and Utter Pradesh. In Maharashtra, most of them settled in Yeotmal district, as well as Parbhani and Nanded district of Marathwada. Some migrated to Chandrapur also. An interesting historical event claimed to be one hundred and fifty years old, was reported from the Manora Tahsil of the Akola district which falls upon the borderline of Yeotmal. One Devba Chauvan, who was a Naik from the Labhan Banjaras went to Hingoli for trading purposes and purchased almost half the area of Hingoli. The local Hatkar community felt that the Labhan will attack them and hence they attacked the Labhans in which Labhans were defeated and had to spread out of Hingoli in the adjacent area.

Russell and Hiralal hypothesise, "that the nucleus of the Banjara caste was constituted by the Charans or Bards of Rajputana," and identifies the Charans and Banjaras quoting Bhimbhai Kirparam. Quoting the monograph of Mr. Cumberlege on the Caste in Berar (presently-Vidarbha), they state that the Banjaras are derived from the Charan or Bhat caste of Rajputana.[2] Believing in Mr. C.R. Crooke's statement that they also mention their first reference in Muhammedan history was found in Sinkandar's attack on Dholpur in A.D. 1504. The Charans or the Bhats have been referred by colonel Todd as, "The bards and the geneologists", and "The Chief carriers of the regions (Marwar), of whom even the Rajput Chiefs were scared. Their *Caravans* or *Tanda* were maintained for carrying food-grains and other trading material as general carriers for the conflicting armies. The Banjaras enjoyed a sort of immunity (comparable to the present Red-Cross) during the wars as they were not attacked or harmed by the conflicting armies — whether Mughal, Rajput or Marathas. These armies purchased grains from them and shifted their camps with the army, along a strong contingent of four to five thousand bullocks and the dogs to safeguard them. Irvin has given graphic description in his, book, *Army of the Indian Mughals*.

The history of migration based on the observations of different authors and their own conceptions and memories of the past as reported in the returns from the Yeotmal Banjaras and those of the adjoining Marathwada district corroborates the tribes migration from the Mewad area of Rajputana.

This historical fact also throws light on the level of acculturation and the beginning of their nomadism. Before migration they were bards and geneologists with a very high level of acculturation similar to the Rajputs. They were graziers and kept cattle, which they continued even after their southward dispersal as traders and suppliers of food-grains. This aspect gave their *Caravan* or *Tanda* the characteristics of a nomadic tribe. In fact, the people from Rajasthan have been migrating to all over India and in all directions and have turned into business community, right from Himalayas to Kanyakumari, and Bengal to Bombay. Those Rajputs who came as warriors and established their Kingdoms in the South held political power like the Sisodiya clan from which Shivaji and the Marathas (like Chauvan, Jadhav etc.) originated. The third significant migration of Rajputs can be observed in the tribal areas of South and even in other tribal tracts where they supplied salt, a scarce commodity for the tribals. They travelled on camels and horses, and not only established friendship but were accepted and got assimilated in those tribes. Examples can be seen among the Korwas, the Korkus and the Gonds etc. They become tribal Chieftans in some areas or, alternatively, established matrimonial relationship at times giving rise to new ruling sub-tribes. The Banjara as a nomadic tribe is also a product of the same migratory characteristic of the people of Rajasthan and as such can not be compared to other tribes or nomadic tribes so far as the original level of acculturation is concerned — whether socio-cultural or economic.

Iravati Karve has said that the Banjaras might have migrated to India from outside.[3] She further states that their names are those of the Rajput and even the marriage rituals simulate the Rajput to some extent. As such, she maintains, they might have migrated to India at the beginning of middle ages along with Rajputs, Gurjars etc. who came to India.

NOTES

1. Nanjudayya, Iyer, K. Ananthakrishna, *The Mysore Tribes and Caste*, Vol. I, Mysore, 1928, p. 136.

2. Russell, R.V. and Hiralal, *Tribes and Castes, and the Central Provinces of India*, Vol. II, Cosmo, Delhi, 1975, pp. 165-67.
3. Karve, Iravati, *Marathi Lokanchi Sanskriti*; R.G. Deshmukh and Co., Pune, 1962, (2nd Ed.), p. 123.

CHAPTER II

SOCIAL ORGANISATION

The Caste Structure

THE SOCIAL stratification of the Banjara from the Mysore/Karnataka side has been stated as under.[1]

Calling it a caste structure, they have been shown to have three major divisions viz.

the Mathuria	–	from Muttra i.e. *Mathura*.
the Labhans	–	Salt carriers from *Gaud* Brahmins.
the Charans	–	found in Mysore, their wandering habits have changed.
the Charans	–	include the Banjara proper under which come *Rathod, Pamhar* (i.e. *Pawar*) *Chauvan*, and the *Vadatiya* Sub-division.
Dhadi - *Tamburi* or *Turi*	–	are Muhammedan by religion.
Sonar (Smiths)	–	Prepare jewels for Banjara Women.
Navi (Hajam)	–	or barbers.
Dhalia	–	Correspond to Madigas - prepare Drums, - they are divided in four exogamous groups viz. Bhukiya, Pamhar (Pawar) Chauhan and Vadatiya.

The Bhukiya are sub-divided into *Jangi* (Khola) having 14 divisions and *Bhangi* having 13 divisions. *Pamhar* has 12 divisions, Chavhan - 6 divisions and Vadtiya has 13 divisions. The Tamburis have six exogamous divisions.

Sub-Group/Castes

Other classification mentions the following major sub-groups/castes.

Mathuria Banjara – equated with Brahmin caste.

Labhana	–	equated with Vaishya caste.
Gor-Banjara or *Charan*	–	equated with Rajput i.e. Kshatriya caste.
Dhadi	–	equated with *Bhats*.
Ravalia Garashiya Pattha		those engaged in bravery.
Rangda Ghetla Jangad		engaged in lower jobs.
Sure-Royado	–	those who kill the pigs.

Among the *Gor Banjara* six sub-castes have been given:

(1) Bhukiya	(4) Pawar
(2) Balnot	(5) Vadatiya
(3) Chavan	(6) Tunwar.

Bhukiyas are also called Rathod. The Mysore Gazetteer mentions four important sub-groups viz.[2]

(i) Bhukiya, (ii) Pawar, (iii) Chavan, and (iv) Vadatiya.

The Bhukiyas are also called *Bada-Rathod* and the Balnots are called *Chota-Rathod*.

In the Vidarbha area and particularly in Yeotmal district, which has got a very high concentration of Banjaras, the major sub-castes reported include, Mathura (Mathuria), Charan Banjara, Labhan and Dhale Banjara. The term Dhale is derived from Dhol *drum* so Dhale Banjara meaning the drum beaters of the Banjara community. In some parts of the area the Banjara are alternatively called *Gormati* (Probably a colloquial form of Gor-Banjara) There are also some *Sonar* Banjara (Sonar means a goldsmith).

Muhammedan Influence

The Turkia and Mukeri have also been reported as two Muhammedan sections of the Banjaras, though both these names contained the same Rajput class names as those in the Hindu sections. This does not mean that these sections could be originally Muhammedan but Russell and Hiralal sound convincing, when they state that some Banjaras may have "embraced Islam under the proselytising influence of Aurangzeb, or simply owing to their having been employed with the Muhammedan troops". The Banjaras have figured in history from the days of Muhammad Tughlak (A.D. 1340) to those of Aurangzeb, as carriers of grains for their armies. However, the great bulk of the Banjaras in the central and southern India, are Hindus, "and there seems no reason for assuming that their origin was Muhammedan".

The Sikh Banjara

The influence of Guru Nanak seems to have affected the Banjaras, as some Banjaras call themselves Sikhs. Mr. Balfour mentions that the Charan Banjaras say that their ancestors were three Rajput boys who followed Guru Nanak. However, the Sikh traditions are not predominant except a few minor customs like a bride-groom tying a rupee in his turban at the time of marriage in the honour of Guru Nanak.

The Clans among the Banjara

There are different class/septs in the castes. The Mathuria Banjara have four clans, viz. Pandey, Dubey, Tiwari and Choubey. They are strict vegetarians. They also recite the Gayatri Mantra.

Among the Dhadi, there are twelve (12) clans:

> (1) Tajnath, (2) Pochala, (3) Ratna, (4) Dungroth, (5) Shara (6) Rudha, (7) Baji, (8) Sagrawat, (9) Bhimla, (10) Bhagrawat, (11) Ramdas, (12) Dehawat.

Marriage between clan numbers 3 to 7 are tabooed.

Among the Bhats, there are twelve clans which are also counted under its equivalent sub-group namely Vadatiya. They are:

> (1) Bhadawat (2) Bori (3) Lakhawat (4) Lonawat (5) Tejawat (6) Dharawat (7) Ghugolad (8) Halawat, (9) Kunsad (10) Malod (11) Ahmera (12) Jetod.

Cumberlege as quoted by Russell and Hiralal also gives four main divisions of the caste in Berar (present Vidarbha), as Charans, Mathurias, Labhans and Dharis.[3] The Charans, who are more in numbers and important among the Banjara are divided into five main clans viz. Rathod, Panwar, Chauhan, Puri and Jadon or Burthia. Each class or sept is divided into a number of sub-septs. Among Rathods the important sub-sept is Bhurkiya, called after the Bhika Rathod, which is again sub-divided into four groups viz. Merji, Mulyasi, Dheda and Khamdar (the groups based on the four sons of Bhika Rathod). The Mathuria Banjaras already referred to above derive their name from Mathura and are supposed to be Brahmins with the sacred-thread ceremony *Mounj*. They are also called *Ahiwasi*. The third division, the Labhans, probably derived their name from *Lavana* i.e. salt which they used to carry from place to place. Another etymology relate, the word *lava* to the son of Lord Ramachandra connecting their lineage to him. They are also considered as Rajputs and the descendants of *Mota* and *Mola*, the cowherd of Lord Krishna. The fourth sub-division, the *dharis* (*Dhadis*) are the bards of the caste, who get the lowest rank. According to their story, their ancestor was a disciple of Guru Nanak (the Sikh Guru) with whom he attended a feast given by Mughal emperor Humanyun. There he ate cow flesh and consequently become a Muhammedan and was circumcised. He worked as a musician at Mughal court. His sons joined the Charans and became the bards of the Banjaras. The Dharis are musicians and mendicants. They worship Saraswati and at their marriages offer a he-goat to *Gagi* and *Gandha*, the two sons of original *bhat* who become Muhammedan.

From the Pusad tahsil of Yeotmal district, where both the sub-groups of Rathods viz; the Bada-Rathod and the Chota-Rathod are present the following clans are reported:

Bada-Rathod: (1) Khola, (2) Ratla, (3) Khatrot, (4) Gedavat. (5) Raslinya (6) Didawat.

Chota-Rathod: (1) Meghwat, (2) Gheghawat, (3) Ralsot (4) Ramawat (5) Khelkhawat (6) Manlot (7) Harawat (8) Tolawat (9) Dudhawat (10) Sangawat (11) Patolot.

These two types are from the Charan Banjara, alternatively called *Gormati* in the area. Another set of clans reported from the area are as follows:

(1) Dharawat, (2) Ghuglot, (3) Badawat. (4) Boda (5) Malod (6) Ajmera, (7) Padya (8) Lakhawat (9) Nulawat.

All the above come under the Jadon *(Jadhav)* Sub-group of the Charan Banjara also called as Gormati in the area.

From the same area among the Labhana Banjara the following clans are reported:

(1) Kesharot (2) Dhirbashi (3) Gugra (4) Rusawat (5) Meghawat (6) Khachkad (7) Pachoria (8) Aalwat (9) Khasawat (10) Bhokan (11) Katkwal (12) Dhobda (13) Machalya (14) Khaseria (15) Gozal (16) Borya (17) Ramawat (18) Bhutiya (19) Bambholya (20) Rethiyo (21) Manzawat.

The Rathod and Jadon from the Charan Banjara are more common in the area. Among the Sonar Banjara Clan names like Medran are found but the type is rare.

A sub-group by name Dhale Banjara (the *Drum*-beater) are also found in the Pusad area having typical clan names, like (1) Hivarale, (2) Karkya (3) Gaikwad (4) Shelar (5) Kamble (6) Deopate (7) Dhawale. These clan names unlike the others given above do not sound akin to Rajput clan names and are similar to those among the Pardhans or other lower castes in the area who are traditionally engaged in drum-beating at the time of marriages or other ceremonies. It is likely that these lower castes were assimilated in the Banjara community as their drum-beaters or the lowest in ranks among the Banjaras adopted the functions along with the clan names/Surnames of the local lower castes engaged in the function.

Rathod is also used as a clan name among the Gormati Banjaras, which is very common. Another common surname is Jadhav which sounds akin to the Maratha surname in Maharashtra.

Medran is a clan name reported from the Sonar Banjaras.

The Lower Castes

Some people among the Banjara are called *Jangad* or *Ghetla* or Rangada (all alternatives for the same), who are treated as *Das* (slaves/servants) and are given a lower status. These are persons who are from outside the Banjara community but are taken in being associated with Kshatriyas and though initially given a lower status, later on may be assimilated in their social organisation.

The Banjaras used to steal away boys and girls from other communities. They either sold them away for a price or kept them as *Jangad* in their *Tandas*. Such *Jangad* girls could also be married within *Tanda* but a Jangad wife was not allowed to put on a silver ornament called *Vakdi* on her foot. Hence she could be easily identified.

Mochi (cobbler) *Mang* (those who take out the skin of dead animals) and *Bangdikar* are other lower castes reported among the Banjaras.

NOTES

1. Nanjudayya, Iyer, K.A.K., *The Mysore Tribes and Castes*, Vol. I, 1928, Mysore, pp. 150-52.
2. *Ibid*.
3. Russell and Hiralal, *Tribes and Castes of the Central Provinces of India*, Cosmo Pub. 1975, Delhi, p. 170.

CHAPTER III

PHYSICAL CULTURE

Physical Features and Appearance

THE BANJARAS are tall, the average being 5′-5″ to 6′ in height in case of men and between 5′ to 5′-5″ in case of women. They are fair complexioned and have a sturdy built. Men are handsome and have a straight nose. Women are beautiful and fair complexioned. Both, men and women have an oval, broad face.

Some of the Banjara particularly the Labhans display blackish skin complexion, but among the Gor-Banjara, the Mathuria and Charan etc., complexion is usually fair.

Anthropometric Indices

	mm
(1) Head (circumference)	530.45
Ratio/cephalic index	77.26
(2) Nose height	177.46
Ratio of length and width of nose.	74.27
(3) Length of upper jaw.	46.86
(4) Ratio of the width of face and head	94.08

The racial characteristics of the Banjara strongly simulate the Aryan race.

Dress

The Banjara men and women have had their traditional dress styles which are still seen in spite of a lot of change in the total life style. Traditionally, the Banjara married women never used the kumkum tilak on their forehead; but of late some women have adopted it.

The traditional dress of the male consists of *Dhoti, Barkasi* and silver *pagdi* (silver-thread turban) and *Shela*. The *dhoti* is worn in a particular manner which is doubly fixed on the waist across the groins and hence is called *Duheri* (double) *Dhoti. Barkasi* consists of a long full-shirt traditionally having twelve ribbons for tying the knots on the chest. Shela or *Dupatta* is long piece of cloth which is put on the shoulders and is usually two metres long. The turban is often in different colours with the lining of silver lace. Due to modernisation, Dhoti and Shirt are the usual dress and the traditional dress is seen among the old persons or on festive occasions/ceremonies. The youths who are educated, use full pant, Manila-shirts etc. and are not easily identified from the youths of other communities and castes.

The traditional dress of the women consists of *Duheri-Lahenga* (a full-size *petticoat* or shirt) *Ghagra* (plated *petticoat* or shirt of large size), a *Kacholi* i.e. a blouse which is often open on the backside and tied by colourful threads or cords, with knots on the back, having cowries and beads and a *Odhani/Dupatta* or a piece of cloth which is placed on the shoulders across the chest and is often thick (*Pomcha*). The clothes are bright coloured, with embroidery with coloured threads and small pieces of glass/mirror enmeshed in it. The pattern reminds us of typical Rajasthani handicrafts. Colour combinations are varied and glamorous with red, green, yellow, blue and black colours predominating. The *Odhani* or shoulder cloth has it's one end tucked in *Ghagra* and the other goes to the head from the back side, covering half the head. Of late, the Banjara girls and Women are using five metre sarees and usual blouse used elsewhere in India, though the traditional dress is still popular and can be easily spotted.

Ornaments

In the Banjara, the ornaments are linked with their dress as well as social customs. Ornaments are of gold and silver but silver ornaments predominate.

The men wear silver earings called *Bali*, and silver anklet on the upper arm *Danda-Kadi*, and a silver belt around the waist.

The ornaments for the women are profuse and are artistically prepared. They are given below limb-wise:

Ear	–	*Zumbar* or *Zumka*
Nose	–	*Nath* (nose ring of gold)
Neck	–	Necklaces and chains of silver or rupees called *Hasali* or *Hār*
Hands	–	Kopra (elbow-rings), Patlya (silver bangles) Ivory bangles or alternatively of lac, horn or coconut shells.

Finger – Ring or *Challa*
Feet – *Kada or Tordya* i.e. silver rings or laces for feet.

A typical ornament which attracts the attention of a stranger is the large bell-shoped ornament tied over the head and hanging down from behind the ears — the big hollow earing, the hollow parts of which are stuffed with sheep's wool dyed red, with lining of small silver bells, and this ornament is called *Zumka*. The anklets on their feet are also hollow with small bells or small stones or balls within which give a tinkling musical sound while walking.

Strings of beads, ten to twenty thick, woven in horse-hair are worn around neck.

The ornaments used by the Mathuria or Labhans are costlier than those of the Charan Banjara. The Labhan girl, when she is ten years of age, is given two small bundles containing grain and nuts which are knotted to the two corners of her *dupatta* (shoulder cloth) and hangs over the shoulder, one in front the other behind. This denotes maiden-hood. These are never removed, and are only removed, to be tucked in the waist at the girl's marriage, where they are worn till death. This practice is not in vogue in Mathuria Women. The married Mathuria women tie their hair straight up, above head and place a small comb in it. A silver chain is tucked in the hair and taking it across the forehead, is kept suspended behind ears. They also suspend a black thread with golden beads from the hair through *tika* (dot of Kumkum) up to nose. Black *Pot* or the *Mangalsutra* is put around neck at marriage. They put on silver rings on fingers of feet after marriage. Unmarried girls are not supposed to put on these ornaments.

A typical ornament indicating a custom among the Banjara is the small, about six to seven inch long horn *Singh* which is called *Chunda*. It is a stick of *Khair* or catechu, and as observed in some areas even two sticks may be used. The stick (s) is placed upright on head within the hair — do and the head-cloth (the *dupatta* or other cloth) is put over it draping over it from sides in a stylish manner. It is also said that the angle of the horn indicates the rank of the women. The front portion of *Dupatta* is called *Ghumto*.

The hair-style of the Banjara women is also a peculiar one. They have their hair hanging down besides the face, on the front side, and are woven in plaits with small silver bells or bright coloured cowries. Coweries are the favourites with the Banjara and are used in dress, ornaments, in houses and also to decorate bullocks.

The ornaments which are of gold, silver and ivory are purchased from market. However, silver ornaments are more common and are usually purchased from markets at Digras (Yeotmal district) and Hingoli (Nanded district). The embroidery work and glass as well as mirror work on *blouses* or *ghagras* etc. is done by the women themselves, thus keeping up the tradition of handicrafts.

The information from the Mysore side indicates that the Mysore Banjara had different names for bangles as given below.

Wooden bangles are called *Bodal*. The ivory or horn bangles on the wrist are called *Bāliya*, and those of ivory or horn, put on the fore-arm are called *Panchela*. Brass anklets are also worn.

Ghugri, Chuda and *Khus* are some typical ornaments which are used by married women only.

The Banjara men also put on a silver ring on right backarm and a silver lac on waist which is called *Kardoda*. They are also using a small silver rod for cleansing ears. *Hukka* i.e. the traditional stand for smoking tobacco and a small purse for keeping betel leaf and betelnuts is always carried.

In the new generation, use of traditional dress and ornaments is going out of vogue, though, in women it is continued in many families except by educated girls.

The substances used for beads, bangles, ring include glass, wood, lac, ivory and brass. The wooden bangle is called *Bodal*. The ivory or bone bangles are called *Balia* and are put on the upper arm. The ivory or bone bangles put on the wrists are called *Panchela*. Usually the bangles on the upper-arm side are nine in number and those on the wrist (number not specified) contain one wooden bangle. One ornament worn around neck is made of squarish metal pieces and is called *Patti*. A thick ring of silver put around the neck with decorative work on the front side is also common. Finger rings are of brass and are seen on palm fingures and also on fingers of foot.

Vakdi a silver ornament worn on the foot of the married Banjara women is not allowed if she is a Jangad woman, and hence such women are easily identified.

Tatooing

Tatooing is common among men and women. The subject matter for tatooing consists of personal name, brother's name or other objects, Gods etc. The common place is the forearm but in case of women, round spots *Tikli* or designs are seen on forehead (near the place where Kumkum or *Tika* is applied) and on nose where nosering is worn. Other objects include scorpion, pair of bullocks, Lord Ram's chariot, Tulsi plant *(occimum religiosa)* etc. The Gods often seen in tatooing include Ram and Laxman, Hanuman, Shri Krishna and Kansa, Vitthal Rukmini etc.

Tatooing has a religious significance but no totemic significance. Such or other signs are not used to identify classes or are not displayed on houses, walls etc. On being asked specific questions on this aspect it was stated that there are no identifying signs/marks/ objects etc. for the clan/sub-groups, nor are these displayed in manners a totem is displayed.

Housing

Their houses are Kuccha houses with mud-walls and bamboo matting. The roofs are thatched, using grass or country roofing tiles or tin sheets. As per their customary concept, living in a pukka or well-built house is considered inauspicious and hence the *kuccha* houses. The floor and court-yard are neatly quoted with cow-dung and mud. The concept is probably related to the nomadic habit due to which only *kuccha* houses were possible and desireable and *pukka* house meant giving-up nomadism and consequently the business.

With the present stationary habits and changes in the occupational structure and education, modernisation has come and such families build pukka houses with slabs etc.

Food Habits

They eat food-grains as well as all kinds of meat. The *Bhagat* does not eat meat. It is also reported that the Mathuria Banjaras don't eat meat and drink liquor. They eat fowls, pork but not beef. In fact, they don't even kill cows and if one kills a cow accidentally he has to go on pilgrimage for six months for purification and should not show his face in the community. This shows their Hindu antecedents. They eat rice and *Jowar* and *Tur dal* (pulse), *Tilli* is easily cultivated by them and *Tilli* oil *(Melia indica)* is used. All vegetables, roots and fruits available in the area are consumed by them. They drink *Mahua* liquor and smoke tobacco through hand-rolled *Bidis*. *Bhang* and *Ganja* is also consumed. Drinking and smoking was very common while going for dacoity or robbery in olden days when they indulged in such activities.

However, even today drinking liquor is common among men and women and it is mostly home-made or is purchased from shops. Though drinking on festivals like Holi, Dussera, Teej and other auspicious occasion is common, even daily consumption is observed. During the present study it was observed that in some households the women are liquor-addict, posing problems for their men-folk. Liquor addiction of men and women is a major problem.

The Banjara are averse to drinking water from rivers, tanks, lakes or wells. They traditionally dig small pot-holes on river bed and drink the percolated water. This habit must have developed during travel through unknown areas where open water could have posed serious health hazards. However, though out-dated, the custom still persists among them.

They are accustomed to tea and consumption of milk is moderate.

It can be observed that there is nothing specific about their food habits and they have adopted the local/regional patterns of food which is natural for a nomadic group and simulates any other rural community.

CHAPTER IV

LIFE CYCLE RITUALS

Birth

ACCORDING TO Banjara custom a married woman never returns to her mother's house and as such her delivery takes place at her husband's place. Of late, she goes to her mother's house but usually the delivery takes place in husband's house only. Impurity is observed after child-birth and as stated by Russell and Hiralal, the mother is unclean for five days when she lives apart in a separate hut in the village. Whether in a moving *Tanda* or a stationary village, this rule of five days is observed, and, on the sixth day she washes the feet of all the children in the village, feeds them and then returns to her home i.e. husband's house.

According to another discription there is a *Pooja* on the fifth day, new clothes are offered to the new mother through five children, and *malas* (garlands) prepared out of wheat are tied on the neck , and on the feet of the mother, and of five children. At a distance from the house holy fire is kindled and other women take the mother upto the place and go on dropping wheat on way upto the holy fire. Wheat is offered as *Prasad*, and a liquid recipe prepared from wheat is given to the mother.

It is reported that a *Dai* (mid-wife) performs the delivery. So far as the impurity of birth is concerned it was reported differently in different returns, the days ranging between 12-13, 37, 40 and upto 6 months. It is also stated that another ritual connected with birth called *Vekalap* or *Natlo* or *Natro* is performed any time upto the forth-coming *Holi* festival. Once this is performed the whole house is purified from the impurity of birth. Thus, it is very likely that the variation in the days of impurity reported depends upon the time-span between the birth and ensuing Holi.

Name-giving

On the fifth day, elderly persons refer to the *Panchang* (Hindu calendar), and give name to the child. The grand-father and grand-mother of the child play a major role in the name-giving ceremony. Name-giving ceremony may be done even after a month. Feast is given to the villagers and tea or liquor is also offered, The feast may be vegetarian or non-vegetarian.

Head-Shaving

The first head-shaving ritual is performed after one year, upto five years. Usually, it is a practice to perform head-shaving of two children simultaneously. Sacrifice is offered on his occasion to the clan Goddess. Some Banjaras worship Lord Balaji on his occasion.

Folk-songs befitting the occasion are sung by ladies in which great deeds of Hindu mythological as well as historical heroes are revived, as if urging the child to become great like them.

Death

The Banjara bury the dead body of unmarried persons and, as a rule, burn the dead bodies of married persons. The death impurity is reported to be observed for three days, while it is also reported as thirteen days. It seems probable that because they were a moving tribe they observe impurities of three days only, as, the ashes are collected on the third day, after which they moved on. Of late, they are relatively more settled in the areas under study and hence they can observe the impurity and relevant ritual process for thirteen days, either as a revival of their old Hindu tradition or as an adoption of the customs of the surrounding community. The process and rituals connected with death are briefly described below.

A pall is prepared with two long bamboos or wooden logs and five small pieces of wood and they are tied together with one unbroken cord. The dead body is bathed with water and placed on the pall wrapped in a white cloth and tied firmly. The son of the dead person leads the funeral procession while relatives and friends carry the pall. Women don't accompany the procession. A coin is tied to the shoulder cloth of the son, which is buried at a distance on the road and the funeral procession proceeds. A pyre is prepared on which the dead body is placed, with head toward North and feet toward the South. The son lits the pyre from the head side. After the body is half-burnt and the bones on the skull are visible, the son touches the skull with a long stick seven times. This ritual is called *Kunchlai* and is considered very important. After burning, the people return and take bath on way back and chew leaves of *Ber* tree *(Ziziphus jujuba)* and spit out. They then console the near relatives of the dead and return home. Meals are not prepared in the home wherein death has occurred and for three days their friends or relatives supply food.

On the third day, the relatives go to the graveyard and collect the ashes and bones and the place of burning is cleaned with water and milk is sprinkled on it.

On the third, fifth, and seventh day different rituals are performed and on the 13th day offerings are given to the dead person and feast given to relatives and friends. This simulates the Tervi (13th day celebrations) of the Hindus. Respect is paid to the departed soul on this day. Non-vegetarian food is also served on this day. Liquor is also consumed.

Shraddha or death anniversary is observed. In the first year this may be performed twice a year or after one year or on occasions like Diwali or Holi festivals. The dead person is considered like God and observation of impurity is not very strict. Another marriage may be performed after next rainy season and a man does not put on his *Pagdi* for six months after his wife's death. Almost all customs and rituals are like Hindus.

Teenage Rituals

Maunj

Among the Mathuria Banjaras who are considered akin to Brahmin and are considered an upper class and have rich living style, *Maunj* i.e. sacred-thread ceremony is performed for the boys. If death occurs, a boy whose Maunj is performed, is burnt and if not, he is buried.

Puberty

After a girl reaches the age of puberty she is required to sit for 7 days at the time of her first manstruation, outside the house in a shade with a roof of leaves. This place is outside the house but within the *Tanda* or *Kudi*. No particular ceremony is observed but leaves of Margosa are stuck on the door of the hut to ward off evils or diseases which are supposed to come during this period. The girl is given a bath on the seventh day, but, is not allowed to go to God's shed for a few more days. Afterwards, during the period in the ensuing month only one or two days impurity is observed and then clothes are changed.

There are no specific rituals connected with the attainment of puberty reported from the area.

Marriage

As per custom, a girl ought to be married at the age of seven or eight years. The boy also used to be relatively young. However, the marriages are now performed between 15 to 18 years of age for girls and between 18 to 21 years for boys. Thus, now, there is no child-marriage.

The marriages are settled by parents.

As a practice, the Naik (traditional head of the village/*Tanda*) is consulted before settling marriages.

Bride-Price

While it was reported that there is no bride-price, in some returns from the Pusad taluq it was reported that amount ranging between Rs. 125 to Rs. 500 is paid as bride-price and Rs. 21 on the occasion of marriage. Four he-calves *Gorhe* are also given, out of which one is to be returned to bridegroom's father after the marriage ceremony is over. In some returns it was reported that half of the expenditure of marriage is shared by the groom's side.

Dowry

Traditionally dowry is not given. However, as per modern development – particularly in the Sonar Banjaras dowry is taken. It was also believed by some respondents that the number of marriageable boys being less, the practice has set-in.

It was reported in all returns that traditionally system of bride-price was present, but is now not in vogue.

Betrothal

The ceremony which is akin a *Sakshagandha* or *Sakharpuda* is called *Gur* (jaggery) in which both the parties and relatives assemble for settling the marriage and *Gur* is distributed. Russell and Hiralal have given the following description of the betrothal from Nemar and Yeotmal.[1]

At a betrothal in Nemar the bridegroom and his friends come and stay in the next village to that of the bride. The two parties meet on the boundary of the village and the bride-price is fixed, ranging from Rs. 200 to Rs. 1000. In Yeotmal, at the time of betrothal, the parties go to a liquor shop and there a betel leaf and a handful of sugar are distributed to every body. Prior to the wedding, the bridegroom goes and stays for a month or so in the house of bride's father, and during this time he must provide a supply of liquor daily for the bride's male relatives. The period was formerly longer, but now extends to a month at the most. While he resides at the bride's house the bridegroom wears a cloth over his head so that his face can not be seen. The boys father sends either a Brahmin or a barber to the girl's father demanding his daughter in marriage for the son. He also informs the Naik of the *Kudi* (village), who calls a meeting of the *Panchas* of different caste and declares the bride-price demanded by girl's father. Both the parties negotiate and after settlement, the *Jasud* (messenger) i.e. the Brahmin or barber returns and informs about the settlement to the boy's father. After the boy's father gives consent, the *Jasud* again communicates it to the girl's father. Then the *Jasud* carries seven pieces each of betel nuts, turmeric rice and kumkum and one rupee as presents to the bridegroom's side accompanied with two men from girl's village, and presents these things to a married women from groom's house who receives it on the shoulder cloth or the ends of a saree put on by her. She examines the present and if found in order, invites all the married women from the village, who sing songs sitting around the plate.

After the songs are over, the presents are taken from the plate. This is the beginning of the ceremony. The betrothal is finalised with a ceremony which consists of worship of Lord *Balaji*, after which the groom's father gives a feast to all the people in the village. Thirteen and half rupees are given to two girls coming from the bride's side and some amount is given to the people in community. With this, the marriage is finally settled and the girl can not be betrothed to anyone else.

The second instalment of bride-price, as settled, is sent to bride's father after which a feast is given to the village community in her village. Later, the pendals are erected at the bride and bride-groom's place in their respective villages.

This information supports the one obtained from the returns, stated earlier and shows the existance of bride-price in the earlier days. Of late, due to introjection, it is slowly receding and dowry in some form is coming up. Though the practice of the bridegroom working as a servant at his father-in-law's place before marriage in lieu of the bride-price, like that of *Dhaglya* or *Lamanya* or *Lamjanya* from same tribal communities is not present, some sort of service as described by Russell and Hiralal must have been there, though in a weak form which was discontinued in course of time. However, presently, such practices are discontinued and hence are not found.

During nomadism, marriages were performed in tents, but with the settled stage they construct a *Mandav/Mandap* (Pandal) with branches of trees and leaves. Previously they used bright coloured cloth — probably to simulate tent. Now it is prepared from branches of *Jamun, Umbar*. A pillar at the centre of the Mandav is made up of *Ganeri*, and *Sag (Teak), Salai, Palas* pillars are made from the stumps of these trees. A central pillar or *mund* is of Kherali, around which the marriage is solemnized. In some returns it was stated that the *mund* is not necessary and the ritual is done near, the branches of Palas tree used for Mandav.

The Marriage Ritual

Prior to the ceremony, the clan God and dead forefathers are worshipped. The specific deities mentioned in different returns include *Jagadamba Devi, Khandoba, Hanuman*, and *Guru Nanak*, the Sikh Guru (mentioned in the return from Labhan Banjara).

Among the Mathuria Banjaras the marriage ritual is broadly of the following type:

On the previous day of marriage the groom is made to sit on a raised platform in the *Mandav* in his house and his sister or sister-in-law or a married woman applies turmeric to his feet and puts *Akshad* (rice soaked in Kumkum or turmeric powder). Then every male member in his family repeats the same and offeres a rupee each as present. Later, the groom is asked to sit on horse's back and along with him men-folk go to the bride's village in a procession. On reaching the bride's place, the bride's father makes arrangement for their stay and immediately sends a shoulder cloth and a pagdi for the groom, which he must put-on immediately. The groom also sends a silk saree, one bead, a bangle and a *Dullad* (a type of necklace). Except Dullad she (bride) puts on every thing. On the next day i.e. the marriage day, the groom goes to the bride's pendal and presents one ornament of beads, a small comb, Sindur, Kumkum and a saree with five small wooden boxes to the bride. Then he sits near the *Homkund* (a squarish altar) for kindling holy fire. In front of him is seated the bride by her father and he gives the bride's hand into the groom's hand, as symbolic of *Kanyadan*. The Brahmin then ties one rupee coin, turmeric and rice in the shoulder cloth of both of them and then ties both shoulder cloths firmly. Both of them move in three rounds around the holy fire and in four rounds around a curtain in the house symbolising *saptapadi* (seven steps) and then sit near the fire changing their places. This is how the marriage is solmenised. Afterwards presents are given to the bride and she is taken to the groom's place which is called *Janosa*.

Another version of the ritual which is given by some respondents runs as follows. A sign of *swastik* is drawn on the back of the groom. On the previous day of marriage holy lights are moved around the face of the groom and on the right shoulder of the groom a mark is created with a heated needle. A feast is given and offerings are made to the forefathers. Near the main pillar of the pendal, on its eastern side, a round pot full of water is placed and pepper, cloves, Jaggery are put in it. It is then covered with a clean cloth and one rupee is kept on it.

On the marriage day the groom takes bath before sun-rise and wears new clothes which is their traditional attire. An embroidered belt on his waist contains a small sword, a javelline on shoulders and sword in the arm pit. A shield is placed on the back. Thus, a dress simulating a warrior is worn and he walks from below the saree which is spread over his head — a saree which is specially brought for the bride. He bows out from below the saree and after coming out of the door a boy and a girl (from different septs) throw Akshad on him. He pays respects to all elderly women and men and sits near a pole *(Khamb or Mund)* which is at the centre of the pendal. Then he presents the saree, blouse, ivory bangles and some sweets to the bride and gives gifts to others. Then, a few steps away his place is fixed, and he is not supposed to return home before marriage.

On the next day he starts with five armed men and after twenty-five steps one rupee is placed which is called *Guru*'s rupee (probably *Guru Nanak* the *Sikh Guru*). This rupee is used for distributing *Prasad* while returning back after marriage. Then they proceed to *Hanuman* Temple and the Naik of bride's village is informed. Then previous agreement is again confirmed and two men take him to bride's pendal. Sweet dinner is served to the groom and his party.

On the next day the bride's father gives a feast to the whole Tanda/village and *Bhang* is offered to all. Turmeric is applied to the forehead of the groom and the bride and *Mounj* is performed symbolically. The groom keeps two rupees in a bowl. Again a feast is given, and a blouse piece and silver bangles are presented to the bride.

On the actual day of the marriage, the bride and the bridegroom observe fast for the day. The actual marriage ritual is performed at night. A few metres away from the home, there is a heap of cowdung. The bride and the bridegroom are taken to the heap, the groom hits the heap with an axe and both of them touch the heap by the toe of the left foot seven times. Returning home, turmeric and *Mehendy* are applied to their bodies, and are given a ceremonial bath. The bride then puts on the saree presented by the groom. He sits in the midst of four pots containing water, jaggery, jawar and wheat respectively. Then, a cotton thread brought by the groom, is used to give seven rounds around the pots and then the rounds are taken away and put around the neck of the bride after giving seven knots to the thread. The same process is repeated for the groom also. Then their clothes are tied and the sacred fire is kindled and sacrifices made. Both of them walk in seven rounds around two pillars together i.e. the groom taking the bride's hand in his hand. Five, round earthen pots with leaves of *Palas* and *Rui* supporting them are placed one over the other, and after the seventh round i.e. *Bhovar* they sit near the pillars. Sweet recipe prepared from wheat flour is given seven times on their hands and they are asked to eat it. Water mixed with rice is placed in a plate and the bride puts a betel-nut, *Kavdi* and rupee in it seven times. The Chord with seven knots tied on the hands of bride and groom is loosened mutually. Then both of them are made to dine in one plate. On the next day, the groom's side hosts a dinner to the Tanda/Village. The bride puts on the ivory bangles and *Ghugri* as signs of married woman. Then they proceed to the groom's place, the bride seated on western side and the groom on the eastern side.

When the knots of the chord are loosened by the bride and groom a song is sung which says:

'Raimal Kanjiro Hatro Bandhno'
'Dore Nakun Chhut Re ladorno'.

This means that the knots tied by Raimal are firm and cannot be loosened. This means the bond of marriage shall last for over. (In the History of Mewad, Raimal was the son of the great Rana Kumbha, and father of Rana Sanga).

The description given above is similar to the Hindu Marriage rituals, particularly from Rajasthan.

Of late, the social part of the ceremony like rice-throwing, singing of *Manglashtak* (eight auspicious songs) and garlanding by the bride and bridegroom multually in the presence of relatives and villagers is also adopted from the (Maharashtra) Vidarbha area. But this is also adopted by many Rajasthani families, who have settled in the Maharashtra area for generations. The performance of the ritual at night is also still in vogue in such families and hence the Banjara customs are very much similar to them. Russell and Hiralal have described the marriage ceremony among the Mathuria Banjaras of Berar (Now Vidarbha) and have said that the ceremony resembles the usual Hindu type. The *Hom* (Holy fire) and the sacrifices after tying knots of the cloths of the couple, and walking around the fire, has been reported by them. They have also described a ritual after the bride arrives at the bridegroom's village after wedding. She fetches water in two small brass vessels, and returns them to the women of the boy's family who mix this water with the water previously stored symbolising the full acceptance or assimilation of the girl in the groom's family i.e. she becomes a Mathuria. Food is then cooked in this water and the bride and the bridegroom are formally received in the bridegroom's village.

Another version of marriage ritual from Yeotmal district is given below:[2]

When a Banjara betrothal is to be made, a betel leaf and a large handful of unrefined sugar are distributed to everybody. The price to be paid for the bride amounts to Rs. 40 and four young bullocks. Prior to the wedding, the bridegroom goes and stays for a month or so in the house of the bride's father. The period was formally longer but now extends to a month at the most. While he resides at the bride's house, he wears a cloth over his head so that his face cannot be seen. The wedding day may be any in the bright fortnight of the month and prior to its celebration they bring branches of eight to ten different trees at night and perform the fire sacrifices with them. For the marriage, 21 new earthen pots are brought from the potters and arranged in four lines with a stake in the centre. The bride and bridegroom sit on each side of this stake, while cold water is poured over the bridegroom's body. Then they stand up and the Brahman clasps their right hands, making them hold a rupee and a cowrie in them and ties a knot in their clothes. Then the bridegroom drags the bride seven or eleven times round the post inside the four lines of pots. The bride pretends to be unwilling, hanging back and sitting down and an old woman comes and prods her from behind to make her go on. The women then put a large plate of rice or meat on the ground and tell the bridegroom to pick it up, standing round and beating him as he attempts to do so. Before her departure, the bride goes round to the houses of her friends and weeps. After the wedding, the bride's father returns to the couple one of the bullocks which he has received as her price. A Brahmin must be employed at marriage, but the Banjaras have caste priests of their own, known as Warthia.

Feast

The most important aspect of the marriage celebrations is a feast/dinner given to the party and the village community. Traditionally, this is non-vegetarian but now it is vegetarian with sweat dishes. However, the poor among the Banjaras still give non-vegetarian dish which costs relatively less. Liquor is consumed profusely and the Banjara dance with songs and music is also performed on the occasion.

Marriage Restrictions

The Banjaras are an endogamous group. They have many sub-tribes or groups simulating caste and certain restrictions were observed between them in relation to marriage. As a tradition, the Mathuria Banjaras did not have marriage relations with the other Banjaras. Among the Bhukiya, Megha and Ratala who come under the Gor-Banjaras, marriages do not take place. In some areas the Balnot and Bhukiya do not have marriage relations. The sub-groups under the Bhukiyas also do not have marriage relations. The Mathuria and the Labhans do not have marriage relations with the Gormati Banjaras and with the Charan Banjaras. In short, even at the sub-tribe or sub-group (or caste level) there is no marriage relationship.

At the clan level there is exogamy. They don't marry within the same clan/sept or *Gotra*. Similarly, certain clans cannot have marriage relationship with certain other clans, for example, within the Pawars, there is no marriage relation between *Zarapala, Vislavat* and *Amgot*.

Though the information returned presents traditions as well as change, it can be easily summarised that there is exogamy at the clan/sept or *Gotra* level, and endogamy at the sub-group as well as tribe level. Certain relations between sub-groups and particular clans are allowed, while others are prohibited. The whole thing must have undergone changes due to the compulsions of nomadism and later due to adoption of modern practices. However, the whole pattern of these relationships represents the same restrictions which are observed in the tribal and non-tribal populations with Hindu traditions.

As per a custom, marriage is possible with maternal uncle or a boy could marry his father's sister's daughter or maternal uncle's daughter. This was reported from *Dhale* and *Sonar* Banjaras.

Re-Marriage

Traditionally, widow-marriage was allowed among the Banjara except the Mathuria. But since long, it has started even among them. In case of remarriage bride-price has to be returned.

After a brother's death, the widow could be married to his younger brother. She could also marry any other person, but that man was supposed to give a feast to the community and seventy-five rupees. However, this custom of marriage with the husband's brother is getting obsolete.

Divorce and Seduction

Either of the spouses can plead for getting a divorce. The case is settled before *panchayat*, and the decision of the *Panchayat* regarding payment etc. (for example returning the bride-price or dowry) can also be taken by the *Panchayat*. The husband or the wife personally appear before the *Panchayat*. A divorced woman can not remarry.

Following account of the Banjara customs on the Mysore side is given.[3] The divorce is very easy. Naik's assent is essential. In case of marriage after divorce, the marriage expenses are paid by the new husband to the previous husband. This include the usual bride-price of Rs. 15 and 3 bullocks and a fine of Rs. 15 to 20 to be paid to caste men if he is responsible for divorce, if not he has to pay only the bride-price.

In cases of seduction of a women, punishment used to be given, which at times was harsh. Now, a fine of Rs. 100 is imposed in lieu of punishment.

At the time of Holi festival, and also when a woman's husband is undergoing imprisonment, peccadilloes (triflings or faults) are ignored.

Widow remarriage is also common.

Family

Traditionally, they have a joint family system with patrilineal descent. The family name continues through the father and the bride goes to the husband's house.

Now, due to division in families or the impact of modernisation and urbanisation, cellular families are also seen. Father is the head of the family.

Relationship within family are based on love affection respect and are depending upon age and position in family. The only relationship which indicates both affection and occasional quarrels is reported between a person's wife and his sister. Parents and the in-laws are held in high respect and similar is the relation with elder brother's sisters etc. Quarrels are common between mother-in-law and daughter-in-law, but the son-in-law commands affection and respect.

Inheritance

Inheritance is through sons and grand-sons, and the daughters do not get share. Panchayat settles all disputes related to inheritance.

Status of Women in Family

The Women are fully engaged in the house hold duties and lookafter the cattle etc. They prepare their clothes, do embroidery works and very rarely work as labourers or on farms. Their role in social and religious functions is extremely limited except the celebrations which are meant for girls and women. They do not accompany the marriage party. Even their role in settling the marriage is negligible. The family finances are also in the hands of men and the women have a limited say in the matter. They are not allowed the participate in the worship of *Seva Bhaya*. Their participation in Panchayats is rare and minimum depending upon the nature of the case. Women are members on the Statutory Panchayat but don't play an active role. Women participate in the dances and they even drink liquor. They freely move outside their Tanda and go on marketing etc.

NOTES

1. R.V. Russel and Hiralal, *Tribes and Castes of the Central Provinces of India*, Cosmo Publication, Delhi, Vol. II, p.173.
2. Govt. of Maharashtra, 1974, *Gazetteer of India*, Yeotmal Districts, pp. 106-107.
3. Nanjudyya, Iyer K.A., 1928, *The Mysore Tribes and Castes*, Vol. I, Mysore, pp. 170-171.

CHAPTER V

FESTIVALS AND WORSHIP

ALL IMPORTANT Hindu Festivals are celebrated. In celebrations, *Wadh-divas* i.e. birthday has also been mentioned in some returns.

An important festival in, *Shrawan* (Hindu month) is called *Teej*. This is a festival of girls and continues for eight days. On the 9th day, two small idols of *Gangaur* and 'Samant' are prepared and worshiped and the girls are awake throughout night. In the morning *Teej* is broken and sapling grown from wheat are distributed.

The *Teej* or *Kajal-Teej* commences on the 3rd day of moonlit (*Shuddha*) half of Shravan month. The girls go to Naik's place. Naik calls the panchas and they permit the girls to sow *Teej*. Wheat are soaked at Naik's place. Unmarried girls and boys go near a *Ber* (*Ziziphus jujuba*) tree and girls take seven rounds around the tree while the boys try to obstruct them. The girls, while trying to complete the rounds, also dig some earth. Then they bring the earth to their respective homes and putting it on small bamboo basket sow wheat on it. On the seventh day from this sowing, a festival named *Thamoli* is celebrated and the *Prasad* is distributed. On the ninth day, an earthen idol named *Kajali-Gangaur* is prepared. Lord Krishna's idol is also prepared and placing them in front of each other, *Pooja* is performed. The girls sing and dance throughout night and early in the morning, before sunrise, they again worship the idols and a few saplings of wheat sown, are taken out and placed on the *Pagdi* of Lord Krishna's idol. After morning breaks, the *Teej* is immersed in water. Then they go from house to house and elderly persons give a rupee or two to the girls. Dance is very popular on the Teej occasion.

Dussera

Dussera is also celebrated, *Ghat* of the Goddess are worshipped for nine days and on the nineth day Goddess *Mahankali* and weapons are worshipped. They used to take these weapons on the *Matachal* mountain but now they just cross the boundary of the village.

Dussera is celebrated by offering worship to *Jagadamba Devi* (Goddess Jagadamba). On that day, black coloured she-goat is sacrificed before the Goddess, and is eaten by all as *Prasad*.

When new food-grains are taken out from farms, these are first offered to the God before they eat it. On this occasion also a goat is sacrificed and this is also called *Dussera*. The prayer or worship songs of the Goddess are sung on the occasion.

It seems that the term Dussera used by Banjaras is not strictly restricted to the Dussera festival celebrated on the Vijaya Dashmi day by the non-tribal and tribal populations in the region, but, in addition to that occasion, the term is also used to celebrate offerings of new farm products as well as sacrifice of animals before the Goddess.

Diwali is celebrated in the usual Hindu manner. Cow is worshipped and offerings are made to Gods and forefathers.

Holi is an important festival. Their new year commences from Holi. They take permission of the Naik one month before Holi and the celebrations start. Singing, dancing , music etc. marks this celebration. If a male child is born in a house during the year a ritual called *Dhund* is performed at the time of Holi. Banjaras from the Bhukiya class are respected on the occasion of Holi. The fire is kindled at the hands of Naik at a place which is already fixed. Then the people go in a group to the house where 'Dhund' is to be celebrated and dance with small sticks in hands keeping the child at the centre. Then all the men and women pray Holi, make offerings of wheat, Jawar and *Tilli* and bow down. After this, a traditional song *Wajna* which describes the battle between Wadatiya and Chauvan clans is sung. Then, a flag of Samant (a forefather of the Chauvans) is hoisted and war games are played. Holi songs (*lengi*) are very popular.

Some minor celebrations include, worship of Balaji on the Gokulashtami day when rice, *khir* and *haluva* are distributed. Similarly on the *Makar Sankrant* day the Naik of the *Tanda* sacrifices a goat and sends small pieces to each house.

Religion and Worship

Gods and Goddesses

In all returns the religion of the Banjaras was mentioned as Hinduism. They supplemented it stating that they were

Hindu-Kshatriya (the warrior caste) Banjaras. Their Gods and Goddesses, mythology, idol worship and animism are also same/similar to Hindus.

The important Gods and Goddesses reported include, Lord Krishna *(Kanhoba), Balaji, Jagdamba-Devi, Mahadev, Khandoba, Samki Mata, Wagha Mai, Hanuman, Sati aai, Sevabhaya*, Mithu Bhukhiya and other Hindu Gods and Goddesses. Along with it mention has been made of *Guru Nanak* and in some returns (from sonar Banjara) of *Peer*.

It is obvious that most of the above names of Gods and Goddesses are the same as that of the Hindus and some Goddesses are given local names which may differ from place to place like that in other Hindu villages.

Jagadamba Devi, Samki Mata, Wagha Mai etc. are all Goddesses and are also worshipped by some Banjaras giving different names like Kalika, Aasawari, Banjari Devi and so on. *Sati* is also worshipped.

It is reported that some fleshy animal (could be a goat or any other) is sacrificed and offered while worshipping the above mentioned Goddesses and *Mithu Bhukiya* and *peer*. For all other Gods sweet rice or other sweets prepared from wheat-flour, milk etc. are offered as *Naivedya* and are distributed as *Prasad*. This means that animal sacrifice is not made before these Gods.

Banjari Devi is usually located in forest and consists of heaps of stones. Smeared with vermilion is a large stone kept at the top of the heap, which represents the Goddess. By way of prayer the Banjaras add a stone upon the heap and pray for protection in the forest. Within the house, a pack-saddle (*Khogir* for luggage) is kept high and used to be worshipped before the Banjara caravan started on their cargo carrying tours. This shows that this deity has an occupational or professional relevance to the nomadic life. It is not surprising that this particular name was not reported in majority of returns because in the present settled life, the other Goddesses mentioned earlier, meant to take care of health and prosperity, or which are local protectors, get priority.

Mithu Bhukiya

Mithu Bhukiya is worshipped as a mark of the age-old tradition of robbery and dacoity in which the Banjaras indulged as an expedient part of their nomadic life. Mithu Bhukiya was considered as a grand ideal in his profession of dacoity. A hut used to be marked in his name in every village with a white flag hoisted before it. The men while starting for an expedition of dacoity will first offer prayers before the hut (there is no idol or any other object) and burn a lamp before it, seeking omen and then proceed on the expedition. Then, they won't speak with each other. On return, a part of the booty will be placed before the hut as Mithu-Bhukia's share, and a feast is given to the *Tanda*/village from it. Women are not allowed to participate in the worship of *Mithu-Bhukia* nor can they enter his hut. These days, the worship is on a low ebb, obviously because it has no relevance to present life as robbery/dacoity are given-up. The reported worship now consists of offering sacrifices of animals and singing *Bhajans*, religious songs etc. before the but.

Seva-Bhaya

A temple was constructed for Seva-Bhaya or *Siva Bhaia* at *Pohur* in Vidarbha, and pilgrims gather in large numbers for worship. The story related to Siva Bhaya which was given by Colonel Mackenzie and reproduced by Russell and Hiralal states that, *Mari-Mata* (Goddess of Cholera) fell in love for the handsome Siva-Bhaya but as he was pre-engaged, he rejected her offer of marriage. As the Goddess was enraged, his wife died and he himself was dispossessed and ruined of every thing. Hence, he surrendered to her and she possessed him giving super-natural power due to which he became a saint and a great brother to all women, but was unable to marry himself. In his old-age the Goddess expressed her desire to marry him and have issue, but he refused and was slained and was buried at Pohur. The Banjars hold him in high esteem and have a practice of taking oath in his name. This incident of Shiva Bhaya is recorded to have happened in 1874 A.D. the name of the person being Siva Rathod.

Guru Nanak

A historical episode conveyed in the form of a story relates to the worship of Guru-Nanak. A Rathod, Pawar and Chauvan had no issue. All the three went to the *Mahakali* temple of Chittorgarh and promised to sacrifice he-buffalo if they be-get sons. Later, they were blessed with sons and the three sent their sons for keeping the promise. The three boys who were about fifteen years of age, fulfilled the promise of sacrifice. The Rajputs considered sacrifice of he-buffalo as bad and hence out-caste the three boys. The three boys left their country and while on way a farmer employed them as farm labourer. They were not accustomed to cutting of trees etc. and hence the farmer ridiculed them, calling them immature and useless *(Gauhar)*. They went away to the jungle and happened to meet Guru Nanak, who consoled them and told them, that they were the 'real' or 'original' using the term 'gorh or Gaur'. Since then, they prefixed the term *Gaur* and went with Guru Nanak to Mathura and he got them married. According to another version Guru Nanak took the boys from Mathura to south. They came across a Brahmin who was worried about the marriage of his daughters. On Nanak's advice, the Brahmin gave his two daughters in marriage to two boys. These marriages were performed on the banks of river *Gorh* and hence the name *Gor*. Thus, the worship of Guru Nanak is associated with the origin of *Gor Banjara*, and also the Mathuria Banjara (coming from *Mathura*). The only custom which now remains is the tying of a rupee in the turban of a bride-groom in honor of Guru Nanak, which is spent for distribution of sweets after the marriage. At present, the Banjaras revere Guru Nanak but have no other rituals or observance. The so-called Sikh Banjara are from this cult. In fact, in these Banjara there is an integration of traditional Hindu worship with the worship of Sikh Gurus.

Worship of Bullock

Bullocks occupy an important role in the occupational life of Banjara as they used to carry loads on bullocks. One bullock, which was not used, for carrying burdens was decorated like a *Nandi-Bail* with silken threads, musical bells etc. and it used to lead the *Tanda* or caravan. For the cure of sickness, for the men or cattle, they used to worship the bull and bow down to it. This bull was never killed as it was considered a great sin. This custom is very natural, considering that the community was dependent upon cattle and bullocks for their subsistence and trade.

Bhagat

In the religious sphere Bhagat assumes importance. He works as a priest, magician and a witch-doctor. Bhagats are classified into, *Guru* and a *Nimbu-Katna* (Lemon cutter) and as a Janta (one who knows).

Guru gives advice regarding religious life and spiritual matters. Some *Gor-Banjaras* even go and stay with the Guru for some days and don't disclose the name of the Guru. The Gurus of the Charan Banjara are from the Bairagis. While some others have their Gurus at the Gurudwara at Nanded.

Bhagat advices about earthly matters and is a worshipper of Lord *Mahadev*. He has a spear, pierced in a lemon, which is used in propitiating the evil spirit. He is a good Bhagat, observes fast and does not consume liquor or meat.

Janta

Janta is a witch-doctor who practises black-magic. The word Janta literally means a wise or cunning man. He uses vermilion, sugar, dates, coconuts, Chironji and sesamum and some oil and performs *Pooja* of spirits and Goddesses controlling diseases and brings cure. He also identifies the witch.

Superstitious beliefs make them believe in black-magic and cure is also sought through it. *Bhanamati* which means a black-magic through which unnatural and unbelievable things happen (like brisk fires without visible cause, shower of stones from nowhere, movements of Chattels etc.) is accepted to be real. *Karni-Kavital* or *Muth-Mama* i.e. the imposition of calamities and diseases on an enemy from the distance through black-magic rituals is also believed in by them. The *Janta* who is a sorcerer helps in mitigating such calamities and relieving of the calamity.

CHAPTER VI

POLITICAL ORGANISATION

The Tanda

THE BANJARAS being a nomadic tribe, could not have an organisation like other settled tribes. They were always migrating and hence the term used for their community unit was *Tanda* which connotes a moving unit. Hence, whatever political organisation worth the name, was not relevant to territorial community but a moving community. As such a feudal or monarchical organisation is not observed. Some Banjaras tell about the Ranas or Rajas of Mewad and Chittorgarh as their kings but this was only historical or mythical. The name of Lakhu Banjara during the Peshwa regime in Maharashtra has been mentioned as their 'chief' in some returns.

The Chief

The Chief of *Tanda* is called Naik and is a presiding authority of the community. He gets a position and honour like that of a king. Below him is a *Karbhari*, then the *Nhavi* and the *Bhat*. These three work under the direction of the Naik, he issues orders which are obeyed by the full community. All disputes, quarrels, problems etc. are referred to the Naik, who gives decisions. He can call the Panchayat and presides over it, and the decisions are of the Panchayat.

During those days when the Banjaras indulged in robbery or dacoity, the Naik used to get two shares, if he participated in the expedition. Similarly, in case a widow married outside her family a fee had to be paid to him. On occasion like *Teej*, the girls go to his place and the 'Naik in Panchayat' permits the commencement of the festival and supplies soaked wheat. At festivals like Holi, Dussera he gets the first honor.

The Panchayat and its Function

The traditional Panchayat consists of the elderly persons from the household presided over by the Naik. They give a listening to the parties and decide the cases. In case of disagreement, panchas from other place may also be called, who can re-decide the case and change or condone the penalty imposed earlier. Usually, the decision of Panchayat is just and accepted by all. The cases settled may include offences, litigations regarding property or inheritance, repayment of loans, adoption, divorce etc.

During the settlement and performance of marriage the Naik and the Panchas have a role, because it is they who declare the bride-price as demanded by the girl's father.

The Banjara Panchayat performs many functions. The terms of settlement of marriage are also fixed in Panchayat. Some statements made by the *Panchas* and discussion indicate the role and sense of responsibility of the *Panchas*. This statement in the Banjari dialect. *"Pachpanchayat Raja Bhojer sabha-Lakhan Savvalakh-Bhair-Anand Samer Kushal-Bhai-apan anand-Saga apan sakal-Talchi patel dhyan-hai to koti Kholu gyan-Nahito panchome Bhagwan-talwa he sansar me bhantbhat ke loksabse halmal chaliya, To nandi nam sanyog-Yeva sagane yeve kariye yeva nandi neer dhapo-dhapsingh siya to jur chadhe seet-yeva sagane yeva najye yevach singoda-Taki log. . . ."*

It means, "This Panchayat of panchas is the *Sabha (Durbar)* of *Raja Bhoj*. The members of this panchayat represent lakhs or one and quarter lakhs of our brothers. I swear by the name of *Talchi Patel* (Tulsi patel) and say that if we remain and think together the God will live in Panchas, the society will progress, like the nexus of rivers. We shall keep our minds clean and moving, if we all come and think together our hearts will be pure, and we shall glitter like a diamond on the crown". The rest of the narrative relates to betrothal.

This paragraph shows how the Banjara traditional panchayat was conscious of its functions and insisted on a consensus arrived at objectively, and full of justice so that the lakhs of their community men would continue to have faith in their panchas. This paragraph reminds us of the traditional speech recited by the elders of the *Kebang* (ancient council) in the NEFA area, collected by Roy and reproduced by Dr. Verrier Elwin.[1]

It is interesting to note that even during nomadism the Banjara remembered their great kings like Raja Bhoj and were conscious of the duty of maintaining the same standards of dispensing justice to their people.

In the settled villages the posts of patel or patil and sarpanch have also been reported. Patil is a traditional post in the rural areas and he may function even as a Police-Patil. In the statutory panchyat, the post of *sarpanch* heading the elected panchayat has been created. Previously, the headman of the Tanda/village used to be a hereditory office, but now the patel and sarpanchas are elected. However, it is observed that the households of the Naik holding the traditional authority got involved in the democratic process and the persons from their families have provided the new democratically elected Chieftainship from the *Gram Panchayat* level up, to *Panchayat Samiti, Zilla-Parishad* and even state level. The present politics of Yeotmal district has been dominated by the Naik family of Pusad providing two Chief-Ministers of Maharashtra viz. Late Sri Vasantrao Naik, and the present Chief Minister Sri Sudhakarrao Naik and other Ministers like Shri Swarupsingh Naik, etc. The names at the lower level also contain many Naiks, which shows that the traditional post-holders got the support of the people in the area, thus providing modern democratic leadership from traditional authority. All the Naiks in present politics have been clever and astute politicians with a development oriented leadership.

Political Consciousness and Participation

Of late, the Banjaras are politically organised and conscious, which is obvious from their participation in the democratic processes and institutions. The men and women turn out for voting in large numbers, and as per returns all persons from a family who have the right to vote, exercise their franchise. In Panchayats and Panchayat Samiti, they participate as members/representatives and this includes Banjara women also. They are active workers of political parties and have many leaders among them. They also participate in organising political movements and propaganda. Many Rathods, Bhanawats and Chavans are working in Political and social sphere in addition to the Naiks already referred to above. Most of the leaders are college educated and other educated Banjaras are in Government service occupying important posts. Their leaders have also established many schools, colleges and technical educational institutions in the area.

NOTE

1. Deogaonkar S.G., *Political Anthropology*, Kitab-Mahal, Allahabad, 1988, pp. 84-85.

CHAPTER VII

SOCIAL CUSTOMS

THERE ARE peculiar customs related to different activities in life. The men folk take meals with their full clothing and *pagdi*, as if they are ready to move out. This custom is related to those days, when they were busy with their expeditions and flight and had to put on their dress even while taking food.

Their drinking habits include profuse consumption of alcohol by men and women alike. This is prepared in homes from Mahua flowers or these days it is purchased from market and consumed daily mostly in the evening. As described earlier it is common to find liquor addicts even among women. On festive and auspicious occasions like marriage, Dussera, Dhund, Teej, Holi etc. alcohol is an essential drink. In response to a question regarding the prohibition law, it was returned from many places that they are just unaware of any such law or that they ignore such restrictions. Consumption of milk is less though tea is a popular drink. Addiction to *Bhang* is also common.

During the good old days, they used to be stationary in the *Kudi* or village, which has a territorial significance. After Dussera they used to move out on expeditions as a *Tanda*, which has a migratory significance indicating a mobile unit. Hence marriages were performed usually during rainy season, i.e. when they were stationary in a Kudi. Even now they consider it auspicious if it rains during marriage.

Drinking water is collected from small, pot holes dug on the banks of the river or from a deep well. They don't drink water which is open i.e. from rivers, lakes and tanks etc. which is considered harmful. During nomadism they must have come across unknown sources of water which could be infected or poisonous and hence percolated water must have been considered safe and hence the custom.

In the chapter on marriage it is already stated, that there is a custom of elder brother's widow marrying younger brother of her husband. Even without a formal marriage she was considered as his wife and their children were considered the children of the decreased elder brother. This was common in the Banjaras from Berar (Vidarbha). Shri Ramu Naik of Koregaon was the first Banjara to oppose, and tried to stop this custom, which is now getting obsolete.

Among the Bhat Banjara, some Muslim customs were followed along with Hindu customs. They had the *Sunta* ritual of the Muhammedans and their marriages were solemnised by Muslim Quazis. These Bhats ate meat, which was uncommon in other Banjara Bhats. In their death ritual a *Fakir* used to perform a ritual called *Fatya*, and then disposed off the body with mixed Hindu-Muslim ritual. These customs are now discontinued.

Shikar

Hunting was a pass-time as well as a mode of livelihood. The Banjaras are traditionally lovers of dog. They had different types of clever hunting dongs. Praised by English officers and authors, these dogs worked as Watch-dogs for the *Tanda* and Cattle and also accompanied them on huntings expeditions. Hunting of wild pigs was considered auspicious. This was called *Aheria*. During an year, atleast one pig must be killed and brought to the Tanda. After showers of rain they traced the tracks of wild pigs from its foot-prints on the wet soil and followed them with the help of dogs. They carried spears and killed the pigs. The man who hit the pig first used to get one additional share, which was called *Surma-Mati*. If the pig bit a dog during hunting, the owner of the dog got one additional share. The Naik of the Tanda got one additional share. One share is offered in the name of Mithu-Bhukia, which is distributed to the Tanda or given to some Nenavat from the Bhukiya household. One share is given to a Chauvan, who holds the flag of the Samanta, and this is done in memory of the historical hero Prithiviraj Chauvan. After the *Shikar* a feast is organised in the jungle and if a passer-by is seen, he is given one share and one more share is given to him for the Naik if his Tanda. If a man is injured during hunt, the Naik takes his care and feeds him till he is cured. According to another version such a hunt may be carried out just with long sticks. It is also stated that the Naik's share consists of the head of the pig, and he may get an additional share also.

Superstitions

Long ago the Banjara particularly the Lambadis were reported to indulge in human sacrifice. In his 'Ethnographic Notes in Southern India', Thurston quotes from Rev. Cains, stating that while starting on a journey they used to procure a child, bury it in the ground upto shoulders, and they used to drive their bullocks over the child, believing that if the child is properly trampled, the journey would be successful.[1]

Another type reported by A. Dubeis, describes that they will abduct the first person they meet and bury him in a hole in the earth upto neck. A lamp made of flour is placed on the head of victim, with four lighted wicks. Then the men and women dance around the victim making great sound until the victim expires. Cumberlege has also reported the statement of a Child who was kidnapped by Banjara Caravan by 1871 from Bhandara district. The child saw, how another child and a woman from outside communities were sacrificed before the idol of a Goddess, with sword, and the blood sprinkled on the Goddess. This child later managed to run away.[2]

The Jungi and Bhangi Naiks accompanied Aasafkhan in 1930 A.D. along with their *Tandas*. In the Charter given to them by Aasafkhan they were permitted maximum three murders in a day in addition to other facilities like water, grass, etc. But the Banjara were believed to be extremely honest and sincere in the work entrusted to them. Of late with modernisation and development and due to discontinuation of traditional work, the above customs have vanished.

Social Reforms

Many social reforms were brought out during the early years of the 20th century due to some well-known social workers from the Banjara community in Vidarbha. For example, late Shri Vasantrao Naik, Shri Babasaheb Naik, Shri Bhanawat, Jatarsing Naik, Rama Naik, Hegappa etc. have to be mentioned as the early workers. Even Sakharam Mude and Shri K.B. Deshmukh who were non-Banjaras also worked hard for reforming the Banjara community. Late Shri Vasantrao Naik had married a girl from a Brahmin family (Miss Ghate of Nagpur) and during those days it was a sensational marriage.

However, late Shri Baliram Hiraman Patil needs special mention as one of the persons who worked for them, though, he himself was from a very poor family. Born at Mahalungi in the Darhwa tahsil in Yeotmal district in 1898, during the Nizam regime, he could not get opportunity for education due to extreme poverty. Even then he passed the fourth primary standard and established contacts with officers in Government and other leaders etc. He came from a village having hardly thirty to forty houses but took initiative by spending five thousand rupees for building a school though people were reluctant to send their wards. By 1936, One hundred and twenty five students were studying in the school, including some girls. Later, he opened a hostel, viz. 'Hira Boarding' for twenty-five students with free lodging, boarding and clothing and books. He even started a library in the town. On the economic front, he started a ginning press at Mandvi and Adilabad respectively, where local people got employment. He expanded and developed his farms and started modern farming. His farm was a model in the district and he himself did manual labour on the farm.

The Banjara women used to wear traditional dress and did not use Kumkum on forehead. Shri Baliramji introduced the Brahmin, Maratha style dresses for women. For such reforms his community out-caste him and even boycotted him. But he continued his efforts, organised lectures, conventions etc. and convinced the Banjara people of the necessities of reform. Thus, he was one of the first social reformers from the Banjara people.

NOTES

1. Russel, Hiralal, *Tribes and Castes of the Central Provinced of India*, Vol. II, Cosmo, Delhi, 1975, pp. 181-182.
2. *Ibid*, p. 182.

CHAPTER VIII

ECONOMY AND DEVELOPMENT

Economic Institutions

SINCE THE Banjara started their nomadic life, their main occupation was supplying food-grains to armies particularly the Mughal army. Hence, either as employees of the army or as traders, they carried on this business. Bullock and cattle were the main instruments of their livelihood. Cattle farming naturally became the second occupation. Another subsidiary occupation was the preparation of Jute-bags and Jute-strings or cords, big needles, wooden tools, etc. which were essential for their main occupation and could be prepared in the household, during spare time.

After the traditional occupation was discontinued and they were settled, they took to agriculture. This was partly due to the fact that with the new sedentary habitat, grazing the cattle became difficult, and hence farming was started as a secondary occupation. But, now some Banjara men and women also work as farm labourers or as workers on development projects etc. The educated among them are employed on white-collared jobs.

Bullocks still occupy important position in their economic structure. But bullock-cart, agricultural implements, and even tractors are mentioned as instruments of production. The Sonar Banjara do the work of Gold-smiths and supply the much needed ornaments to the society and have mentioned as the instruments of production, iron platform, hammer, scissors, forceps, blowing tubes etc. The Dhale Banjara who play instrumental music have mentioned Dafdi, *Tholi, Chatki* as the instruments for earning livelihood.

The above description shows that, they had well-organised economic structure, in which the cottage industry supported their main occupation, but with changes in their nomadic life-style and occupation, new occupation was adopted, which is presently their chief means for subsistence.

During the historical past Brigandage in the form of dacoity and robbery must have been a secondary occupation, as is clear from the worship of *Mithu - Bhukiya*, and some other rituals and customs. This is also confirmed from the fact that during the British regime, they were considered as a criminal tribe and the police kept a watch on their activity. They conducted attacks on wealthy households and even on cattle and the contingent could be as strong as 100 to 150 men, with big sticks. Wealthy travellers were also attacked. Russell and Hiralal have reproduced graphic accounts of such raids originally recorded by Major Gunthrope in his 'Notes on Criminal Tribes Frequenting', Bombay, Berar and the Central provinces (Bombay 1882). But all *tandas* were not necessarily of criminal tendency and showed honesty as transporters or traders.

Development of the Banjara

After Independence the process of democratic planning was started with emphasis on the development of the rural masses in general and the weaker sections in community in particular. The weaker sections included the Scheduled Castes, the Scheduled Tribes, the Nomadic tribes, the Vimukta Jamati and other specified groups. The tribal population attracted the major portion of the schemes, and relatively speaking, the Nomadic tribes started getting benefits at a later stage. However, so far as the Banjaras are concerned their level of acculturation being much higher (as discussed earlier), as compared to the Scheduled Tribes from the same area like the Pardhans, the Gonds, the Kolam's etc., the efforts were forthcoming from the educated and modernised leadership from among the Banjaras. Usually, it is observed that educated persons and modern leaders from the tribal communities travel away physically and mentally from their own group and are thus alienated to their own group. On the contrary, the traditional leadership from the tribes is with their groups, but is hardly development oriented. Significantly, both these draw-backs seem to be conspicuously absent from the Banjara leadership. The educated, modernised leadership worked for the upliftment of their community and such leaders were provided from among their traditional leaders, significantly the Naiks. While on one hand many Banjara villages (a better word to describe their present status as against *Tanda*), have still maintained the socio-cultural and economic pattern including dress, food-habits, customs, social organisation and broadly, even the occupational structure which arose under the settled conditions, on the other hand persons or individuals from these villages rose to high educational and socio-economic and political status, establishing an infrastructure for the welfare of their people. The educational institutions, cooperatives and other organisations established by their leaders are rendering different services to the Banjara community.

Shri Vasantrao Naik Pratishthan which is a public corporation with headquarters at Bombay has given aid for their development.

Among the schemes for their development some schemes were preferred by them and they got the benefits out of such schemes. These include, roofing tiles (Manglore tiles) for huts/houses, I.R.D.P schemes, Anganwadi, seeds and manures for farms, labour work under the EGS (Employment Guarantee Scheme), pairs of bullocks, Bank loans etc. In some returns they also mentioned the Family Planning/Welfare and Adult Education as schemes which reached them. They demanded irrigation for agriculture, Anganwadi/A.N.P (Applied Nutrition Programme) and E.G.S. on large scale. They felt that though their socio-economic conditions and disabilities were similar to those of the Scheduled Tribes population from the district/area, they were not getting similar benefits. The benefits given to them were too less and should be increased.

Education

The Banjaras are known as a brave, hard-working and honest community. Though robbery and dacoity was practised, it was not done by all the Banjaras and many of them carried out their trade with all sincerity and at all costs and facing all odds and risks. Russell and Hiralal have quoted Colonel Makenzie's opinion as under:

> "A Banjara who can read and write is unknown. But their memories, from cultivation, are marvellous and very retentive. They carry in their heads, without slip or mistake, the most varied and complicated transactions and the share of each in such, striking a debtor and creditor account as accurately as the best-kept ledger, while their history and songs are all learnt by heart and transmitted orally from generation to generation".[1]

The present status regarding education is altogether different. Literacy has spread and the new generation in the post-Independance era has been attracted towards education. The Banjara leaders have established educational trusts and institutions of their own, running links of schools, colleges, hostels etc. catering to the educational needs, not only of the Banjara but all the people. The Banjara boys have shown good progress in all faculties including technical and professional education. The list of such institutions is imposing. However, spread of education of Banjara women is low and needs to be encouraged. The developmental machinery of the Government had also provided the infrastructure which has promoted education and development. The Vasantrao Naik Pratishthan Corporation, having its head office at Bombay gives financial and other help for many developmental activities.

NOTE

1. R.V. Russell and Hiralal, *Ibid.*, pp. 191.

CHAPTER IX

THE BANJARA FOLKLORE

Language

THEIR LANGUAGE is called *Banjari* or *Labhani*. It falls in the Austro-Asiatic group of Languages and sounds nearer to Rajasthani languages. Some have opined that it is closer to Gujarati but the folk-literature given in this book shows its nearness to Rajasthani. It has adopted Hindi as well as Marathi terms depending upon proximity of habitat. Though the Banjaras are spread in North India as well as to south upto Mysore there is no significant difference in their language except the knowledge of local/regional language and adoption of a few words. In Mysore area the language is called *Kutni* or *Katni*. *Banjari* is a dialect and there is no specific alphabet though it can be easily and correctly transcribed in Devnagri script. However, it is rich in folk-literature, particularly in folk-songs and also folklore.

Population by Banjari language for Yeotmal district from each Taluka (1961 Census)[1]

District/Taluka	Area	Male	Female
Yeotmal	Total	53,131	50,187
	Rural	52,839	50,065
	Urban	292	192
Darvha Taluka	Total	19,738	18,383
	Rural	19,678	18,373
	Urban	60	10
Pusad Taluka	Total	25,153	24,210
	Rural	24,960	24,104
	Urban	193	106
Kelapur Taluka	Total	5,718	5,425
	Rural	5,707	5,425
	Urban	11	—

The comparative position of language is as follows[2]:

Language	Percentage to Total Population				
Census:	1901	1951	1961	1971	1981
Banjari	7.72	9.56	9.40	N.A.	N.A.

Banjari has the second largest number of speakers in Yeotmal district. Its speakers account for 9.4 of the total population of the district. It is spoken more in rural areas where its speakers are as much as 10.7 per cent.

Dance and Music

The Banjara dances are colourful and grandeurous. These are community dances and are performed in groups of girls, boys, men and women, either separately or in groups. Hairstyles and hair-do, costumes, ornaments etc. are artistically done using bright colours.

Dances are performed on various occasions like marriage, *Dhund*, sowing of wheat, and on festivals like *Teej, Holi, Dasmi* (*Dussera*), *Gokulashtami, Balaji-Saptah* (Balaji-week), *Durga Utsav* etc. Some dances are of specific type and are given specific names; for example:

Occasion		Type of dance
Holi	–	Sarvajanik payee (community stepping)
Teej	–	Langdi payee (Twisted-feet stepping)
Marriage	–	Sarvajanik Zanjkali (Daud) (Community Brisk dance with Zanj)
Durga Utsav	–	*Tipri Nritya* (Dance with small sticks)

They compose the songs themselves and sing on the occasion. Traditionally composed songs may also be repeated with or without changes. There are no separate poets or composers of songs. Singing is also on a community basis. Hence singing and dancing is a community entertainment similar to other tribes in the area. The songs are befitting the occasion or festival and may contain reference to Gods and Goddesses, mythical and historical heros, while others are philosophical in nature. These are preserved and handed over by oral tradition and new dimensions, themes are added according to the changing environmental context, (Please see following on 'Folk-literature' for details of songs).

At times historical events are replayed as dance-dramas like *Dandhar* (term usually used to describe similar forms of this performing art in Vidarbha). The author had an occasion to witness one such dance-drama on the life and deeds of the historical hero, Bajaba Naik, which was performed very effectively by Banjara folk-artists.

Musical Instruments

Their musical instruments include *Dafdi. Tholi, Chatki, Zanj, Lezim, Nagara* (Drum), *Dodpayee* etc.

In some returns *Bhangda* and Band were also mentioned as musical instruments. Band means the side-drums or the traditional *Dhol* which is beaten by sticks on both sides. Bhangda should be a type of dance than a musical instrument.

Dodpayee is an instrument which is used when the women dance. Some of the instruments are prepared within the *Kudi* or *Tanda* locally, from the skin of buffalo and goats. Other instruments are purchased from market.

Folk-Songs and Folk-Tales

Marriage Songs

The songs traditionally sung at the time of marriage are very rich in their content and represent a variety of sentiments as well as themes.

These could be tentatively grouped into *Mehandi* songs, *Tandgir* (Turmeric) songs, songs related to bride-price, jokular or teasing songs, parting songs and blessing songs.

The lulling songs *(Lory)* form another important category. The mother's love for child, her ambitions and pangs are also displayed.

The sowing songs are also an important group of songs sung in groups by women while sowing seeds in farms. The themes cover a broad range of subjects from family problems to philosophical truths.

The prayer songs or *Inti* (called *Aarti* in Hindi) are also common in the folk-literature. *Inti* can also mean a request.

The worship songs include the songs sung while grinding,

Bhajans, narrating stories of Gods and on Saints.

Festival songs are for festive occasion particularly Holi (*Lengi*-songs), *Nagpanchmi*, etc.

Povada and other assorted songs form the last type.

Mehandi Songs

While grinding Mehandi for marriage this song is sung.

Mendi dal mendi dal chay lada,
leriya pisa dichik koni re,
Aadlim pisa e jiva kasa |1|
Khoto pisa chalenire,
Bana pisar, rani malenire |2|
leriya pisa dichik kone re . . .

We are grinding Mehandi for marriage, does the wolf give money or not. (wolf indicates the groom). Our mind is like money in a measuring pot. As counterfeit coins don't work, so also bride cannot be obtained without money. Does the wolf pay money or not.

The above song shows the existence of the practice of bride-price.

Tangdir Song

This is a marriage song which is sung while applying turmeric to the body of a bride.

Chhodiyake aai yadis,
Ek ghadi lageto, so ghadi,
lagyach yadi |1|
More ke batlari chunkeri chavodi,
Chavodis hidu yorodis |2|
Mariyeke virenaro libuvaro bag,
limbu aam todi yarodis |3|

Mother you have left me at my husband's place, I am feeling one minute as one hundred minutes.

My father's drawing room/office is well built, I stroll in it (I feel like returning to take a stroll in his room).

My brother's garden is full of lemon trees, I feel like coming to the garden and plucking lemons in the garden.

This song depicts the mind of a married girl, who though in her husband's house often remembers her parents, brother etc.

A Rhyme at Feast

Before marriage, the contract of marriage is affirmed in the presence of both parties and then a feast is given. Just before dinner starts the following rhyme is loudly sung by a man.

Rada- Meethi Ghodli
Ran- Meethi Talwar |1|
Sej- Meethi Kamini
Sura- Meethi sang |2|
Lo Bhai Bhang - . . .

A mare is liked by a warrier (Radha — a brave man or warrier), a woman is liked while going to bed, a sword is liked while going for hunting/war, similarly O' friends! treat this feast as dear to you and start taking food and Bhang.

A Mantra

While giving a mark on the shoulder of the bride-groom before marriage the following Mantra is enchanted seven times.

Koli aava koli jaav
Koli Bhai Jag samav
Dholo Ghodi Ḥanslo
Patliyo aasvar
Munge aavda mogre
Talli aavda Bān
Guru Baba, Sada Sada Jaan

There is a custom, among the Banjara of tying a (Gartani) black cord or black beads on the leg below knee of an unmarried girl. Before taking the bride to marriage pandal, this is removed. The following song is sung by the bride on that occasion.

Gartani mat todo jamne
Todo Kavarane Kakroso
Mār virāri hateri

Gartani mat Todo
Sererei seravi
Gartani mat todo

Oh friend or sister (who is removing the cord) please don't remove that black cord (*Gartani*). Why are you breaking it? Why are you sending me away from our house? Please don't break the Gartani tied by the hands of my brother.

On the occasion of marriage a sister sings the following song:

Vira mote sherem jau kair
Vira nav mal haldi mol laukair
Vira Husheti haldi lagau kair
Vira mote sherem jau kair |1|
Vira navmal sakharya lan kair
Vira gundi laduri panyat Warudu kair
Vira navmal kuku lau kair
Vira Husheti kuku lagan kair |2|

At her brother's marriage the sister sings this song. She says, "Shall I go to the market and bring nine mounds of turmeric and apply it to your body?" Again she asks, "shall I bring nine mounds sugar from market and serve *Bundi ladoo* (sweet balls) at the marriage feast?" Lastly she asks, "shall I fetch nine mounds of Kumkum from market for your marriage?"

Turmeric, sugar and *ladoo* as well as Kumkum are all auspicious things at marriage and the unit of nine mounds also indicates her auspicious blessings, as number 'nine' is supposed to be an auspicious figure in the Hindus.

Ji Chalo Mandap Me

Some one is being persuaded to accompany to the marriage pandal for feast and things are being described.

Bijali gyaski lagiye rosli,
Udra aabiy gulal jibem chalo
mandao me |1|
Shir shobhe sevalkhaki kanthi
Kanthi bot hajar ji chalo
mandap me |2|

Shir shobhe seva lakhaki bajya
Bajya bot hajar ji chalo
mandap me |3|
Shir shobha seva lakhaki kapada
kapada bot hajar ji chalo
mandap me |4|
Bajya bot hajar ji chalo
mandap me.
Shir sobhe seva lakhaki dagina
Dagina bot hajar ji chalo
mandap me |5|
Bajye bot hajarji chab mandap me

Light from electricity of gas (petromax) are put on, and, *Gulal* (pink powder) has spread in air, let us go to marriage pandal.

On the neck is a neck lace worth thousand rupees, clothes on body are of thousand rupees, and ornaments are worth one lakhs and quarter rupees, let us go to pandal. The band is being played in the pandal.

Bayaro Song

This song is sung at the time of marriage.

Matyake karoy nayaka yadi,
yadi dek bapu dakay laju mar nakore,
lakopati jiveda. |1|
Aadi revot aageli pori ravot, pichedi yadi. |2|
Aala modi, khula modi, kul modi,
Hathem zari len paniyan jau yadi. |3|

Oh, Naik mother, see how I am shy of father, my life is of lakhs worth.

Ahead of me there are many girls and behind me also there are girls, and behind me is my mother.

My style of walking is unique. I am going to bring water with a pot for water.

Ladi Beti

This song shows how a fondled daughter is demanding things at her marriage.

Ladi beti tebalpar rumal mange,
Uska bapbhi rupya hajar mange,
Uski mayebi sola sangar mange,
Ladi beti tebalpar kapada mange,
Uski mayebi sola sangar mange,
Uski mayebi sola sangar mange,
Mandvas betho Javai, bot pyara lage
Chchoti saliro behnoi, ghunghat waliro nalandoi,
Chhoti sali mange, shirni dono javai.

The fondled daughter is asking for a handkerchief on table.

Her father is also demanding thousand rupees.

Her mother is also demanding sola-shringar (sixteen traditional beauty aids used by a married woman).

The fondled daughter is asking for a table-cloth.

Her father demands thousand rupees and mother sola-shringar.

The son-in-law sitting in the pandal looks very sweet and loving.

His wife's younger sister (*choti sali*) and his wife's brother's wife who has taken *Ghungat* (Cover on head and face) are asking for sweets from son-in-law.

Kishorilal ki Ladki

The song shows how one Kishorilal has lovingly brought up his daughter.

Kishorilal ki ladki, kishorilalse
pyari,
Matane dudhāse pāli, pitane
phandume dali,
Pita lego, pita lego, dali ki raj
behangaonko,
lai lungki lakdi, banai hej ki
khichadi,
Dekho jat ki masati,
Pita lego-pita lego, dali ki raj
behanganko.

Kishorilal loves his daughter more than himself. Her mother gave her milk and father safeguarded her.

She was given the sticks of clove and *Khichdi* (a recipe) of a cereal to eat. See the grace of the tribe.

In this song Hindi words are used along with Banjari words.

Bansiki Aawajko

It is a lyrical song showing a girl's attraction to her proposed bride-groom.

Bansike aawajko to, mai bagume
Sunithi,
Mai to sun rahi thi, mai to dul
rahi thi, |1|
Bansi kaiko bejyar,
Mai to tikit kad rahi thi, mai to
paise zok rahi thi, |2|
Bensi katheko bejyar,
Bansi ke aawaj ko to mai motar me
sun rahi thi,
Bansi kaheko bejyar. |3|

I was listening to the tunes of flute in garden, I was moving to its tune, why do you play on flute?

I was purchasing a ticket and I was paying money, why do you play on flute?

I was listening to the tunes of flute while sitting in a motor (car/bus) why do you play on flute?

The purport of the song is that she was attracted to the groom all the while whether in garden, on journey, and why should he attract her so much.

While going to her husband's house after marriage the bride says:

Choot giyaye mari Bapuri haveli,
Khayeshi piveshi nangri.
Mari Nayak bapuri nangri,
Gujrathni yadi, umriyav Bāpu,
Kesariya Viranna,
Haveli choodiyali yadi.

I am leaving my father's house, let them get ample food and drinks, or, the house where I was well-fed is being left by me . I am leaving our Naik's village. My mother is a Gujarathan (a lady from Gujarath) father is an *Umrao*, my brother is a brave *Kesariya* and I am leaving all of them.

While blessing a bride for becoming a mother the following song is sung.

Dharito Mandan Meliya,
Vanshero Mandom soot |1|
Taneri Mandan Tariya,
Baputiro Mandan poot |2|
Jalam Des Mata,
Samant soor veer |3|
Nito reejo Mata vanzdi,
Mat gamav jo makhl rao Noor |4|
Veer Des Mata samant soor,
Par mulkhon-par Kam sadhare,
Taro nam Raja dhares |5|

The earth's decoration is cloud, similarly a son is the decoration of a family or race. As a women is decoration for a body (man), a son is a decoration for father. Oh' mother, give birth to such a son who will be brave and great, or else, remain barren, and don't lose your face. Give birth to such a brave son who will rule other countries.

Ab Jamana Palat Gayo

In a jockular way the song introduces the bride to new relatives and their relationship.

Pena chandi ke rupaya chalate the,
Aake chalo kagatiya Jamana,
Aab Jamana Palat gayo |1|

Pahele sasrese sasubai darati thi
Aabi daro sasuji, aab jamana palat gayo |2|

Pahele Jetse Jethani darati thi
Aabi daro Jethani, aab Jamana palat gayo |3|

Pahele derse dervanibai darti thi
Aabi daro dervanibai, aab Jamana
palat gayo |4|

Previously, silver rupees were used now paper currency has come, the era has changed.

Previously, the mother-in-law was afraid of father-in-law now she scolds him. The era has changed.

Previously, husband's elder brother's wife was afraid of him, now she scolds him. The era has changed.

Previously, husband's younger brother's wife was afraid of him, now she scolds him. The era has changed.

Lory Songs

At the time of name-giving ceremony or at the *Vekalap* or *Natlo/Natro* ritual connected with child-birth referred to earlier, the following song is sung by ladies.

Pelo nam Swamori le syan,
Swameero jayo anand badayo |1|
Dusroye nam Mahelyaro le syan,
Mahlyaro jayo anad badayo |2|
Tisroye nam Dhartiyo le syan,
Dhartiro jayo anand badayo |3|
Too bhalo jalmiye Kesriya Rajpoot,
Tare angan galras amblo |4|
Too bhalo jalmiye Arjun sarikhe bir,
Tare angan galras amblo |5|
Too bhalo jalmiyo Ravaliyake Rajput
Tare angan galras amblo |6|

Prayer is offered to Gods like Swami, Mallhar (Shiva), the earth, and then, the child is called with the names of heroic persons like Kesariya Rajput, Arjun, Ravaliya Rajput etc; and offered blessings.

Lory (Lulling Songs)

This is a lulling song sung while a child is sleeping.

Zujubala Zujure, gogo duk lopo du
Zija sidadu massuro bag lagodh Keloro,
Hatam dandiya sojero bala sojor, |1|
Halo karuk palo karu bala rov jeti Kaso Karu. |2|

Harur gular khetwadi bala suto Zujawadi,
Tar thadi gicha haten lai kacha kodi bala
so jar |3|
Halo baba halo dhorumai chalo suko
dalya khalo,
Kulbyari bhandi madi tare gharep sankadi |4|

Oh child, sleep in the cradle. Shall I give you jaggery or coconut? Shall I stich a shirt for you or plant a garden of bananas for you? I shall put a gold ring on your hand, please sleep.

I am rocking your cradle for long but you are not sleeping, so what shall I do?

Your mother kept you on the farm and has gone to bazar, and she will bring a *Kavdi* (Shell) for you, please sleep.

After rocking your cradle I shall go to farm and give you wheat flour, please sleep.

The houses of the *kunbis* are well-built (*Madi*) but you are under a thatched roof, so please sleep.

Another Lory Song

Halo halo karagi Zolim sawargi,
Kai dago degi balem baiye. |1|

Namdeo bala galiti kar chalaye,
Mare balam jijan topiye
Toi maro bala samjeni baiye. |2|

Tare balan dudheri kacholiye
Toi taro bala samjeni baiye. |3|

Aadoshi padoshir najar lagichaye,
Nud marchyari najor kadaiye,
Toi taro bala samjeni baiye. |4|

Soner chendu chandir dando hatem
Toi taro bala samjeni baiye |5|

His (child's) mother rocked the cradle and went away to the farm missing his eye.

Namdeo bal (another child by name Namdeo) plays in the street, and my child has a shirt and cap (purporting to say that Namdeo has not), even then why my child is crying, I don't understand !

I have given milk to your child in a bowl, I don't understand why your child is still crying?

I thought, the bad looks of the neighbours have affected you, I used salt and chillies to remove the bad effect of the 'look' (Drishta i.e. Najar), even then your child is crying.

Your child has got a ball of gold and has a silver ring on wrist, even then the child does not stop crying.

These, lory or lulling songs are like other songs sung in Maharashtra for lulling children to sleep. In fact, the subject matter of these songs is not for the child, as it is too young to understand the words or meaning. It is the lulling tune in which these are sung by mothers or other ladies which lulls the child to sleep. The things said in these songs show the thoughts which occur to the ladies who sing. Their earthly ambitions, longings, prospects for the child etc. are reflected in these songs. The Banjara women are no exception to these sentiments prevalent all over the region.

Sowing Songs

The women work on farms. During the sowing season they sing songs while sowing is in progress. Some songs are given below:

Jalman Kai kamai mari mataye
pan phul wai gamaiye.
Vor aasturin latay kapada
Matan chitari vitaye.
Vori aasturin ghodep basaro,
Matan paidal chalaye.
Aangeshi malgoye akanarashi,
Ghodlep besewalo kulye.
Ghodlep besewali ora aasturi
paidal chalewali mataye.
Vori matan silepale takdaye
Vori aasturin shiram puri.

By giving birth what could the mother earn? Leaves and flowers were wasted. The wife gets a new cloth while a mother gets torn pieces of cloth. His wife gets a horse to ride while mother walks on foot. While walking he met a man who asked, "who is sitting on the horse ?" Reply came that the horse rider was his wife while the pedestrian was his mother. Stale food for the mother and sweets to wife.

This song equates mother with mother earth by giving examples from social life.

Song Sung While Sowing Seeds

Baiye soyak guliro dhado mandocha
Katven padiye chor,
Baiye dhade hundyaga tokalo padocha,
Baiye tokaler upar vatala padocha,
Baiye tokaler upar vatalo padocha,
Jharire upar galo padocha,
Katven padiye chor.
Baiye tokler hundyaga bhala gadocha,
Katven padiye chor.
Baiye bhalati abu jhabu bandecha,
Katven padiye chor.

Oh sister, a pandal of strong mat (Bamboo mat) or canvass is constructed, how can a thief enter ? Oh sister, a big utensil *(Gund)* has been kept and on it is placed *Zari* (a big spoon) and a disc is placed on its mouth. How can a thief come ? Near the utensil is kept a javelin and two dogs are sitting near it. How can a thief come ?

The song purports to predict good crop of paddy and no thefts.

A Sowing Song

Mundo dinoye ton mito bolen,
Sar dan karlo kam baiye.
Ghadibhar bhajalo Ram baiye,
Ramero nam setiye moto.
Chheni kasero toto ye,
Mundo dinoye ton moti bolen
Koni.
Dinoye ton vaita bolen,
Hat dinoye ton dharam karen,
Dino koniye to bhata marenye,
Sari dan karlo kam mari baiye,

Ghadi bhar bhajalo Ramye,
Dola dinoye ton duniya dekhen,
Koni dinoye ton dola maren,
Pag dinoye ton pap karen,
Dino koniye ton pap karan,
Valkan dekhalo sarmar baiye.
Zuto chhe sab sararlol
Sevabhaya,
Saran valko Tukaram bowa,
Chalego dolir mai sam rararlol
Sevabhaya,
Valkan dekhalo sarmar baiye
Zueto chhe sab sararlol sevabhaya.
Soran valki Meerayebai
Pachai jerer pelarlol Sevabhaya
Valkam dekhola sarmar baiye
Zuto chhe sab sararlol Sevabhaya
Saren valki Janayebai,
Dev ona chakki chalayer lol
Sevebhaya,
Valkan dekhalo sarmar baiye
Zueto chhe sab sararlol sevabhaya
Soran valki Pralhad bala
Chalego evainem mair lol
Sevabhaya
Valkan dekhalo sarmar baiye
Zueto chhe sab sararlol
Sevabhaya.

Mouth has been given by God for speaking sweet words. Do hard work throughout the day and utter God's name. For a moment take god's name, Ram's name is great. If you utter his name there is no loss. Mouth has been given for talking nice words and not bad words. The hands are given for giving alms not for throwing stones. Oh, sister, work throughout the day and utter Ram's name. Eyes have been given for seeing this world and not for winking years at others. Feet are given for pilgrimage not for doing sins. *Sevadas Bhagwan* (God Sevadas) could know all this and the fallacy of earthly life and went away. Saint Tukaram sat in a palanquin and left this world while alive, but this earthly life is perishable.

Oh sister, this world is false and Seva Bhaya could recognise this fact. Saint Meera Bai could digest even poison, Seva Bhagwan and Saint Janabai could recognise these facts. The God helped Janabai in grinding grains and Gora Kumbhar was assisted by the God in preparing earthen-ware posts as he had recognised these facts. Oh, sister, do understand that this visible world is Maya (false). Bhakta Prahlad recognised this fact and was saved by God by sending an aeroplane. Seva Bhaya and others knew the falasy of this world.

This is a philosophical song which tells the women to develop the right and objective approach to earthly life. It refers to many saints whom the God helped in overcoming the hurdles in earthly life. It refers to Saint Meera Bai and Seva Bhaya who were naturally well - known to the Banjara even as nomads. However, the references to saints Tukaram, Janabai, Gora Kumbhar etc. who were worshippers of Lord Vithoba (at Pandharapur — in western Maharashtra) indicate a strong influence of the *Varkari Cult* on the Banjara community. This may be due to the settled life they are leading in Vidarbha area.

In Praise of Lord Vitthal

Yeki vitep hubo Vithoda,
Kai ton bhaktiri godir Vithoba,
Gorya Kumbhare ghar garo khundarochi,
Jana katalo koni aayor Vithoda.
Kai ton bhaktiri godir Vithoda
Bhim Arjuneri Jodir Vithoda
Yeki vitep hubo Vithoba,
Gorya Kumbhareghar pali bharichi,
Kai ton bhakriti godir Vithoba,
Bhim Arjuneri Jodir Vithoba.
Yeki vitep hubo Vithoba,
Gorya Kumbhareghar pali bharichi,
Kai ton bhaktiri godir Vithoba,
Bhim Arjuneri Jodir Vithoba.

Oh, Lord Vitthal, (Vithoba) you are standing on one brick and you like worship. When you went to Gora Kumbhar (Kumbhar — an earthen potmaker) and helped in mixing mud. You like worship *(Bhakti)* very much. Bhim and Arjun's brotherhood is reflected in you. You are standing on one brick. You did even water-service at Gora Kumbhar's place. Oh, Vithoba your nexus with worship is like the unbreakable brotherhood of Bhim and Arjun. This song also depicts the influence of *Varkari* cult a worship orientation of the Banjaras.

Ganpatis Aarti

This is a worship song in praise of Lord Ganesh.

Jay Ganapati Swami Ganapati, tu ghan nila,
tu sundewala Oavalacha ton aarti.
Undarep besan aajo Ganesha tari nameri
hamnen aasha,
A bal teri gadi laga desh,
aadi vot paraya mat,
rukayes balatar Udabatti, Karacha tari
Bhakti |1|
Mahadever hatem kamaler lota, hatem
trishul mathepar jata,
Aaye jo vihnen utlo tu hata tare
namese garochu gatha,
Mata tar parbati shubhchvor pati |2|
Tu Ganpati ganero dātā, tāre nāmer
vat vata tare uparaicha hamari satta,
Kakmara ton premeti kavi Tukari Bhakti |3|
tu ghannila tu sundewala oavala too aarti,

Lord Ganpati you have trunk and blue colour, I praise you and move holy lights around you.

You come by sitting on rat we have hopes in your name, if you clear my path, I shall offer incense to you and perform your Pooja, and worship. Oh, blue coloured God with a trunk, I worship and sing in your praise.

Lord Mahadeo (Shiva) has a lotus in one hand and a trident (Trishul) in another hand and has large plaits of hair on his head, and he is your father. If your reverse our calamities we shall sing your stories. Your mother is Parvati whose husband is Lord Mahadeo. Oh, God Ganapati, I move these holy lights around you. Oh, Ganesh, you are the giver to all, even to the illiterates those who read your *Geeta* (stories and praise) get knowledge and become intelligent.

We are calling you with love and we claim your blessings. Poet Tukari worships the blue coloured God with a trunk.

In all Hindu worship and religious rituals, Lord Ganesh is the first God to be worshipped and it is believed that he saves from calamities and give knowledge and intelligence. The same ideas are contained in this praise song. The only new thing is the blue colour ascribed to Ganesh, which is queer, as, normally vermillion colour is ascribed tc Him.

Worship Songs Inti (Aarti)

This *Aarti* of Goddess Jagadamba is sung on Dussera occasion. It is sung in group.

Jay Jay Jagdambadevi yadi vaghepar
savar vegi,
Hatem aasul lidi nagar vasatin sai va sukhi.
Gaudhanen sai va bal bal moti salgar
rakad,
Karaktem barkat kar jat samar vot ghor va,
Bal Bal moti salangar rakad,
Kani Kani badhat bani rakad.
Chite vat phatte kar, padi rotikhad kar,
Dhav Jen par aasha bandir aasha pur
karlan.
Jay Jay kar rakad yadi,
Tar namer puja hui jakol,
Sen sai vatu,
Tare makanem puchato vejav.

Oh, Goddess *Jagadamba Devi Mata* you are sitting on a tiger and have taken a whip in one hand. Please give happiness to all, let my cattle and cows increase and let me prosper. Give, victory to us and bread to eat. Let all our hopes be fulfilled. May your name, worship and fame spread, we have come to your temple to praise you.

Guru Nanak's Inti (Aarti)

The Banjara worship the Sikh Guru Nanak. This worship song is in praise of Guru Nanak.

Jay Jay Guru Nanakji Guru Nanakji,
Sangeet boloji, bagru karktem barkat kar,
Jat samro vot ghor va jay guruji
gangayadi,

Bal Bal moti salangar rakad
Dhav Jen pav, saroto savvasher
karalulu
Satya bat phattya karku,
Jay Jay vay guru, jay guru Nanakaji,
Jay Guru, Jay guru jay guruji,
Tare namero bhog lago,
Jankol Nanded puchat vejav.

Guru Nanakji your praise and fame may spread and increase. Give us prosperity, let my belongings be doubled. Let truth be proved and upheld. I praise you and offer you *bhog* (offerings and puja) at your shrine at Nanded (at Gurudwara at Nanded).

Song Sung while Grinding on Grinding Stones (*Janabai's Song*)

Janabain ghati pisaye
Kai ton bhaktiri godi Vithoba
Bhim Arjuneri jodir Vithoba.
Janabair dhonlo dhoyachi,
Jan katalo koni aayor Vithoba.
Kai ton bhaktiri godir Vithoba,
Bhim Arjuneri jodir Vithoba.
Janabair sada nakechi,
Jana Katalo koni aayor Vithoba.
Kai ton bhaktir godir Vithoba,
Bhim arjuneri jodir Vithoba.

Oh, Vithoba, how much you like worship. You helped Janabai in grinding grains. Bhima and Arjuna are a pair incarnating love. When you helped Janabai in grinding, you were not tired, so how much you like your worship and worshipper ! Bhima and Arjuna are inseparable pair. You even sprinkled water in the courtyard of Janabai's house, but you were not tired. How much you like your worshipper is clear from it.

Bhim and Arjun are a pair of unbreakable brotherhood and so is your love.

Rām and Seeta Song

This song puts forth a metaphor showing how the God who lives in every soul behaves on this earth leaving the original traits.

Ram bes rel sita bes motar,
Sita phado maro shree Bhagwan.
Ram khave poori, Sita khabve shira,
Kai khawe maro shree Bhagwan ye
jivaler rejem.
Khurchip beto maro shree Bhagwan,
Kai aiytiti chal maro shree Bhagwan.
Ram khave supari, to Sita khave lung,
Kai khayo maro shree bhagwan ye
jivaler rajem.
Gal tulasir mal sodun gele Ram Ram.

Ram sits in railway train and *Seeta mata* (mother Seeta) sits in a car and the tickets are issued by my *God* (Bhagwant). Ram eats *poori** and Seeta eats *Sira**, so many things are eaten by my God on this earth. The God sits on chair. Ram eats betel-nut and Seeta eats clove, when my God Ram takes birth on this earth he eats and does many things and leaves here *Tulsimala**.

Draupadi Vastraharan

In this song based on Mahabharata epic, Draupadi is calling Lord Krishna for help.

Hakarure kana virela kalakaliti,
Bhari sabhamai hubire kanavirela.
Man kavar gher lidere kanavirela,
Mar ejjat rakadre kanavirela.
Man sadi puradare kanavirela,
Oan antakarneti hakarure kanaavirela,
Gadi Duarkati aajore kanavirela.

Draupadi: Oh Lord Shrikrishna (Kana-Krishna and Virela-Brother) I call you most earnestly for help. I am standing alone in a

---

- *Poori* – a fried recipe from wheat flour
- *Sira* – a sweet, prepared from wheat flour
- *Tulsimala* – Garlands of occimum religiosa.

Sabha (*Durbar*) full of people and the Kauravas have enclosed me.

Oh, *Kana Dada* preserve my modesty and prestige.

Oh, Kana Dada supply saree to me. I am calling you from the bottom of my heart, so, please come as early as possible from Dwarka.

This song shows a strong impact of Hindu epic Mahabharata and worship of Lord Krishna among the Banjara.

Song in Praise of Lord Vithoba

Soneri Vitep Hubore Vitthala Pandharin beto,
Bel phuleri mal laire Vitthala develem beto,
Pedha, narel laire vitthala develem beto,
Janabain ghati pisaye Vitthala devlem beto,
Meerabain jer pachayer Vitthala raulem beto,
Savata malin bhaji khudaye Vitthala, devlem beto
Gorya Kumbharen gara khundyo
Vitthala, Pandharim beto,
Bhaktim bala khundayo Vitthala,
Pandharim beto,
Tare bhakten payore Vitthala,
Pandharim beto,
Ham kair chori kider Vitthala Pandharim beto.

At Pandharpur Lord Vitthal is standing on a brick of gold. Oh, Vitthal I have a garland of *Bel* and flowers for you,

Oh, Vitthal, I have come in your temple with *Pedhas* (Sweet prepared out of milk cheese) and coconut.

You helped Janabai on grinding-stone. Due to you Meerabai could digest poison, You helped Savta Mali in plucking vegetables.

By sitting in Pandharpur, you also helped Gora Kumbhar in mixing mud, and he trampled his own child in mud while engrossed in your worship.

You always came down to help your worshippers, then what theft (i.e. wrong) we have committed so that you are not blessing us ?

Vitthala (Incarnation of Lord Vishnu or Shrikrishna) at Pandharpur is the famous deity of lakhs of people from Maharashtra and the seat of Varkari cult. The saints referred to above are all worshipped and their *Bhajans* (worship songs) are sung by all masses in rural Maharashtra including Vidarbha area. The Banjara who show a Rajasthan origin and came to Maharashtra and settled in parts of Vidarbha seem to have been impressed by the Varkari cult and become worshippers of Lord Vitthala which shows how integration takes place.

Near Yeotmal district, on the Nanded (Marathwada) side is a hill at Mahur on which the old, historical shrine of Renuka-Devi is installed. There is also a temple of Anusuya Mata from the Dattatraya legend. This Shrine is worshipped by thousands of devotees from Maharashtra. The Banjara people also worship the Goddess and visit it.

Song on Anusuya Mata

Anusuya yadi nahalen beti,
Nahaleti lai jamburi doli.
Sigrep bal ghiyari holi,
Dattaye bapu nahalen beto.
Nahaleti layo Jamburi doli,
Oh ! Mohrem ! bali ghiyeri holi.

Godders Anusuya Mata is taking bath, A branch of Jamun tree has been brought for her bath. On your (Goddess) peak a holy fire of ghee is burning. Lord Dattatraya is also taking bath. A branch of *Jamun* is also brought for his bath. Holi fire of ghee is burning on the peak of the Mahur-Gad.

Festival Songs

Bal Rich Holi (*lengi songs*)

This is one more song on playing Holi.

Mahur padep bal rich holi,
Mahur padep bal rich holi,
Anushya karmeli khir-poli,
Dattaro bala ramro holi,
Pandharpuram balrich holi |1|
Rukmina karmeli khir-poli,
Vithalero bala ramro holi,
Pohra gadem balrich holi
Pohra gadem balrich holi |2|
Dharmeli karmeli khir poli
Bhimaro seva ramer holi. |3|

Holi is being played at Mahur, Goddess Anusuya has prepared *Khir* and *Poli* (*Khir* a sweet in milk and Chapati of wheat flour) and Lord Dattatraya is playing holi.

At Pandharpur holi is played, Goddess Rukmini prepared Khir-poli and God Vitthal is playing Holi. At Pohra Gad Holi is played, Goddess Dharmeli prepared Khir-poli and seva Bhima is playing Holi.

This is an attempt to involve all Gods and Goddesses in their joys at the time of Holi festival.

Holi Songs

Some one is calling all to play the throwing of colours at the Holi festival.

Adore daysani holir khela,
Bar minam aair holi holi
Khelor Zoketi |1|
Holi khelore Rām jalam dinor,
Holi khelor zoket |2|

Come all old people, Holi comes after twelve months, so, let us play Holi, Let us play it at leisure.

Ram has given us birth let us play Holi.

Holi Song

Kale pile phetiya valiye ton baba balav,
Bava balav ton nachano shikav,
Nachano shikav ton hasano shikav
Hasano shikav ton rovano shikav
Aadi pori ratero tandore lado |1|
Batuna rego malan batuna led ra,
O, batuvam lung, sapari Ora galane har,
Batuwa dhunden chali geryatali lndo devar,
Dhund dhundan vore kholem ghalo
Chatkan chumo ora gore gal. |2|

(1) You are sitting, wearing a black yellow *Ghagra* (plated petticoat), you are called by your father. He wants to teach you

dancing and singing. If you accompany us then only you will come to know that he will teach you dance and singing.

(2) At midnight the *Tanda* is marching. But her purse has been forgotten somewhere behind, clove, betelnut and her necklacc are in that purse. To search the purse she has gone with her loving *Devar* (husband's brother). He searched her purse and gave it to her and forcefully kissed her fair cheek.

This song refers to Saint Sevalal who left Pohra-gad.

Kai chhodor gorun sevalatol,
Pohragad vase pado |1|
Hapa vadun sobtam lido,
Hole gararya sadairi dholi havori,
Pohragad vase pado |2|
Navse gharen sobtem lido,
Kai ladeni lador Sevalala,
Pohra gad vase pado. |3|

Why did you leave Pohra-Gad (Pohra hill), Oh, Seva lal, why did you leave the Gor Banjara?

Your brother also left with the cows and bulls and Pohra hill was deserted.

You left with persons from nine hundred houses vacating pohra hill, and Oh, Sevalal your town Pohra Gad was deserted (Sevalal refers to Seva Bhaya).

Lengi Songs

These songs are sung at the time of Holi

Sevan jata doi Holi ramacha
Ori sagula mar tukarire,
Bhimaro seva ramaro Holi |1|
Raman lachmal holi Ramacha,
Hanuman maro tukarire,
Dashratha ro chhora ramar holi,
Parsharam bole abhola garjacha,
Renuka bole vij kadkacha,
Mari peteri bemari hoye sarkacha,
Mari peteri bemari hote sarkacha |2|

Dattatri bole Abal garjacha,
Ori Anusaya bole vij kadkacha,
Mari matari bemari hoto sarkacha |3|
Pandurang bole Atal garjacha,
Ori Rukmina Bole vij Kadkacha,
Mari Rukmina bole vij Kadkacha,
Pandurnag bole Abal garjacha
Ori Rukmina bole vij kadkocha
Mari Puteri bemari hote sarkacha |4|
Sewabyaya bole Abal garjacha,
Sagula a bole vij kadkacha,
Mari chatiri bemari hote sarkacha. |5|

They sing songs on the occasion of Holi and enjoy.

Ram Laxman and Hanuman enjoy Holi festival. The sky roars with Parshuram's name and lightening shines in Renuka's name.

The disease in my stomach has come to my lips i.e. is going away. Again the same is repeated in the names of Dattatraya and Anusuya and it is related to relief from diseases. Pandurang (Vitthal) and Rukmini, Seva Bhaya etc. all are remembered comparing to roaring of sky and lightening and stating that my body is being relieved of disease due to those Godess and Goddesses.

Lengi

Sat bhaveti dhoko, dev paichyare sat bhaveti,
Bhav rakadi yet bholi Meerabair,
Uto jerero pela pachai prabho |1|
Bhav rakado yek Goroba kamarar,
Vitthal kan mara gara khundaye prabho |2|
Ran nam bhajoto Pralhad balen,
Lale khambeti mungi chadayo prabho |3|
Bhav rakodo yek Savata malo,
Dev lan bhaji khudayo prabho |4|
Kero Rathod ye chha santeri wanir,
Bhata tarange palire maire,
Sat bhaveti dhoko,
dev paichyare sat bhaveti |5|

If you have true/real faith the:

(1) God blesses you and obliges you, Meerabai had real faith, her poison was digested by God,
(2) Gora Kumbhar had faith and true worship, Vitthal helped him in mixing mud.
(3) Prahlad had real faith so God came out of pillar.
(4) Savta Mali had real faith, so God plucked vegetables in his garden,
(5) Poet Rathod says that with these six saint's words, Bhats can reach the banks of this river of life.

Lengi (Holi) Song

Samka mata deram dhud nakar samkavo mata,
Zirmir Zirmir pali padchar,
Kichdem gavadi phasacha bhayara,
Sewalal kero vo badubhainar,
Jalu lago umari gaden badure.
Badubhai Jaro vo umeri gadner,
Hamkaro Tukaramen bhayare,
Tukaram hakmaro majur loknur,
Chalo jao Povara gadem bhayare,
Navase gharerire navase chhorire
chali aao bhayare derare bhaire,
Tukaramerire samki chhorir,
Dhone palim vela lagicha bhayare,
Samka mata deram dhud nakar Samkavo mato.

Samka mata was on a hill at Umari, it was difficult to go on foot and carts used to stuck up in mud. Tukaram called the labourer brothers to go to Pohara hill where there is other seat of Samka mata, and fulfil the promised worships at her shrine.

Changonabai Song

Changonavobai mahadev ton saiye changonovabai,
Brahma, Vishnu, Mahesh tinar,
Chale aao changonare ghar devre,
Zari khakol pali dini devenar,
Besen palang rolai prabho.

Tin deve kere vo changona matanar,
Bhuk lagari hamen mataya.
Pacha prakar chhattis bhojanar,
Aao dev bęso bhojanen prabho.
Koni khanva changona aaso bhojan,
Chilvyaro banad bhojan baiye,
Changonorobaiye mahadeo ton saiye changonovobai.

The song is based on the famous tale of Chilaya Bal of Changuna. Brahma, Vishnu and Mahesh (Siva) went to Changunas place and sat on a cot and asked for meals. She prepared five types and thirty-six meals for them, but Mahadeo asked Changona to prepare meals by killing her child Chilaya.
(The song, as obtained, is incomplete)

Lengi Songs

This song is based on the epic tale of Raja Harischandra who was famous for his bounties. It also shows Lord Shanidevas influence.

Hari Chanderaja sapnem dan dino hari chand raja
Narad muni hate mai vina jhalnar,
Hari chander uto gun garo
Ris aaicha vo Shanidevenar,
chalo aaro mirat lokum prabho,
Shanidev hanaro vagha banayaro,
Vedo ghalo aavadhya nagaren prabho.
Nagarir lok kere hari chandenar,
Hamnen vagha sataro rajare,
Harichand Tararani jare doi venar,
Dabalege voi vaghen prabho,
Hari chande raja sapnem dam dino hari chand raja.

King Harischandra give *dān* (gift in alms) in his dream. Naradmuni praised him. Lord Shanidev created a tiger and made him move in Ayodhya town. The people of Ayodhya said that tiger is troubling them. Raja Harischandra and Rani Taramati came to the rescue and controlled the tiger.

Holi Song on Krishna

Her path is blocked by Krishna while she was going to Mathura.

Rum Zum Rum Zum, chali Mathuran,
Shirpar dahiro mat, bhai bhaire,
Shirper dahiro mat,
Chhodar Krishna chhodar mur ari
Jayad Mathurau,
Ghar kal Jovaro vat,
Tare balan dudhero pela,
aat tu karad mukkam,
bhai bhaire aat tu karad mukkam,
Tiki tiki tekadip vasali vajay,
regir vanem sari rat,
bhai bhaire regir vanem sari rat.
Chhodar Krishna jayad gharen,
Ghar mare sasareri dhak,
Tare sasaren ganjero hoka,
aat tu karad mukkam,
Bhai bhaire aat tu karad mukkan,
Chhodar Krishana jayad gharen,
Ghar mari sasuri dhak,
Ratbhar karad mukkam,
Patlishi aat tu karad mukkam,
Ghar mare patiri dhak,
Tare patin daruro pela,
Mare kan karad mukkam.

She was going to Mathura, the bells in her feet (*Ghungroo*) were tinkling - *Rum-Zum*. On her head was a bowl of curds, She says "Oh, Murari (Krishna), let me go to Mathura, don't block my way.

He says, "your child has drunk milk, so you stay here today"

She says, "you are playing on flute the whole night in jungle, let me go, I am afraid of my father-in-law".

He says, "the father-in-law must be smoking *Ganja* on his *Hukka*, so you stay here for the day".

She says, "she is afraid of her mother-in-law and hence must go".

He says, "your mother-in-law must be eating pan (Betel leaves) and hence you can stay here for to-night".

She says, "Let me go as I am afraid of my husband".

He says, "Your husband must be down with glasses of liquor, hence you stay here to-night".

Thus she goes on persuading Krishna giving reasons for going to Mathura and Krishna turns down all excuses given by her and asks her to stay for the night.

The song shows strong worship of Krishna and cultural links with Mathura.

Bhang

Bhang is the indegenous narcotic which is popular in the Banjara, on occasions.

> *Bhang ye bhang, Jhalatali bhang,*
> *Kore kapdem chhang,*
> *Bhang miti ram miti,*
> *chadata bhang aasman kar,*
> *Utarati bhang panchemkar,*
> *Vetdu beto Jyaneti bhangloo maneti.*

Bhang is taken after putting on new clothes. *Bhang* takes a man, high up in the sky when it seduces brain, and when it recedes, the man comes down to normalcy. The people are addicts of Bhang.

Ghota (Bhang)

> *Jat Bhukiyaro beta, kad kastunbo ghota ghole,*
> *ghota mele panch, keni pucho na pucho,*
> *Bakshis karo bha.*

A son of Bhukiya Banjara caste grinds the *Bhang* (Ghota), you will get five bowls of Bhang, whether ask or don't ask, but give Bakshis (gift) to him.

Got

> *Het mel tin mangala upar mel pipa,*
> *Dhagadhagda angpar salge, Jale gher ka khunt,*
> *Chuye mandari bund, ye movdari khir lapsi,*
> *Yej movdari daru, keni pela navala/puche na puche,*
> *Aanga anga dali, lar lar kali,*
> *Pucho no pucho karo bakshis.*

A tin of drum is kept on a three brick furnace (*Chulla*) in which logs of wood are burning. The Maḥua liquor being prepared in it is like a *khir* (a semi-liquid drink). Whoever, drinks the Mahua liquor which reaches all parts of his body and gives pleasure which can not be described. Give *Bakshis* for supplying and serving it.

This is a song putting a puzzle and then providing an answer to it:

Question: *Bole re koriya kagad*
Bol re hari thala be,
Besneki dhadki bandu, pineki zari bandu,
Khaneki thali bandu, ye aarteri arth ka,
Tater beta pach bhojan kho.

Answer: *Vad kature vedi thali katu,*
Katu Vader geta lu
Satha vapder khalu ladu,
Opar baladu ridi,
Upar melu zari, zarip gelu thali,
Aang beti dai sali, lar beti ghugatwali
Chhodad pancpuri thali, bankar khais de thali

Question: Oh blank paper for which purpose shall I use you? for tying edibles, or as water bowl on plate.

Answer: The answer comes that sweets be kept in the pot, which be tied with the bowl on it and then all put together.

Raja-Bhoj's Panchayat

Pan panchait Raj Bhojer cha bha,
Bhain sak pachare jag yeketi yek sawai,
Pachare lakha aal pachare lok sawalakha,
Sati Kiya mejawani kiya sati nakta bada,
Sarat bhando soma bhangi sali nakta,
bada sangero ghar Jada. |1|
Chuno kahe mail charko-charko,
Jangal ka raja jalan sari rat,
Kato kahe mai kadwa-kadwa,
Kadwa humari jat,
Lung kahe mai pet patola,
Mat Jhalariya top chari kan barabar,

Jayphala kahe mai parmal bhari,
Doda kahe mai chhattar dhari,
Jispar chhattar chhaya voi pasare hāt,
Supari kahe mai khardi-baradi,
Sab rang hamare pas,
Vetadu hudo jhaneti ranga saga lo Maneti. |2|

Panchas assembled in Raja Bhojer panchayat, every one was great and competent, lakhs of people had assembled. All dined together. Chuna, lavang, Jaiphal, Kath and Doda, supari having their own peculiarities were brought together to give a different colour. So, also the panchas gave a special colour to the Raja Bhoja's Panchayat.

Nagpanchami Song

Virela kabse khadire dukanpar,
Virela hasalo darare tare rajem,
Virela bapuri killi tari hatem,
Virela hasalo darare tare rajem,
Virela ghalan hindi tare bagem,
Virela kabase khadire dukanpar,
Virela bhuriya darare tare rajam,
Virela ghalan Hindu tare bagem,
Virela ghalan Hindu tare rajem,
Virela kabase khadire dukanpar,
Virela lowadi darare tare rajem,
Virela odan hindu tare bagem,
Virela odan hindure tare rajem,

Baiye viran meli posadem,
baiye baretali jou ori vataye,
Baiye sutebutero Oro thato ye,
baiye bapun meli posaden,
baiye daselagu Jou Ori vatye
baiye redu ghadiro Oro thatye,
bapu posaden gom boli koni,
bapu lovadi laye m boli koni,
Virela bare minaro san aayore,
Virela bain balau aayore,
Virela baisaru lowadi layore,
Virela lowdi pasand koni aaire,

Virela lowdi huseli layore,
Virela bhavaj dekcha risetire.

This is a song purported to be sung by a sister asking her brother to do several things for her.

Brother I am awaiting for a long time in your shop.

Brother, you please buy a neck-ring with beads.

Father's safe's keys are with you, so brother let me purchase beads.

With those beads around my neck, I shall stroll in your garden.

Brother, I am waiting in your shop for a long time. Please purchase a nose ring for me. With that nose-ring *(Nath)* on my nose I shall move in your garden.

Brother you give me a shoulder cloth *(Odni)* I shall wear it and move in your garden.

Oh, sister, we shall send our brother to the bazar at Pusad and wait for him till twelve O'clock.

Oh, sister, brother has put a suit and is wearing shoes and is showing off his personality.

Oh, sister, we shall send brother to Pusad and await for him till 10, o' clock. He likes Radio, Watch. Father went to Pusad but I could not talk to him.

Father brought a shoulder cloth but I don't say any thing.

Oh, brother, this festival comes only once in twelve months, so, go and bring sister. Purchase clothes for her. Brother has very gladly brought clothes for her (sister) so how can she not like the clothes. But, brother's wife is looking at me angrily.

Nagpanchami being an important festival, married girls come to father's house and usually the brother goes to bring them. The girl, then tries to persuade brother for giving her gifts. The song nicely depicts the general sentiment of sisters towards brothers, father etc.

Povada and Other Songs

Povada is a typical folk-song sung by the *Shahirs* (Poet-cum-singers) in a particular manner accompanied by a group of singers who repeat the last line of every verse.

A Povada which is believed to be composed by Vasya Dhadi Banjara is given below, The Gor Banjara of Vidarbha still sing this Povada. It refers to the Seva Bhaiya i.e. the Seva Naik Banjara who was killed by enemy and his elder brother Waghya took revenge on enemy.

Povada

Satguru Samaru Sharda
Saraswatin Dhavun,
Deva Sharadan dhavur dhaun,
Ma kanthema Saraswati Bol.
Hardo kholan gaun |1|

Lavadiya Seva, Majla Dar Majla,
Tanda landlore,
Lavadiya Majla Ladiyo,
Sirpen Aayo Parbatin Aayo
Devgaden Aayore |2|

Deogadro Deoraja, Rajan Balayo,
Lavadiya seva, raja Balayo Darbanre,
Narsi pethro gavari komti boliyo,
Samal Seva Baat, A jateri Talikha,
Jo Chavaneri Jat re,
Lavadiya seva, Talo khajo bavan,
kalti re; |3|

Seva Nayak Boliyo,
Samal Maari Baat,
Gamera Ghetla Vat re vat,
Rajputere Gharema Janam liyo,
Veereroch ghatman, sureroch opman,
Raghughar Janam liyo,
Koni Manu Baat,
Gamera Vani, Dhum Machayun,
Bavan kaltire |4|

Udachanda Vadtiya,
Dhalur kot banayo,
Barchhar Megh Barasayo
Goliro Mar lagayo,
At jer Dhadi sammat Puriya,
Kosu Bhadkayor,
Dhadi ro Beta,

Sirpada Hariya Bagemare,
Seva Nayak saman, kalad,
Duniya kachh Aachho,
Sansar kach Aacho,
Raghghar Janam liyo,
Pag na diyo pacho,
Lavadiya seva dhoom machayo,
Bavan kaltire |5|

Sevan khabar lagi,
Waghan padgo ghor,
Chado waghla joreti,
Padi nangra dhol,
Raghuro wagha,
Ban chadech ranjitrore,
Chado Waghla Jorti,
Ghodi parti aav,
Sinduda chadto aav,
Tukari padti aavre aav,
lar samant halke aavre |6|

Ek din ek ratema parbhati,
Aan maloyo Raghur Wagha,
Aan malayo narsi pethemare,
Paravtiro kollo fodo, mati todo,
Ghalo lavadiya ghero,
Ek din, ek ratma
Sevar ver fero,
Raghuro wagha, ver lilayo,
Seva-Nayakero |7|

Mahanadi Matreti aai,
Aad aayo poor,
Gangamai aai, poor re poor
Bavan paada vadtiya,
Too jaais katreek door, re,
Mahanadi mat rati aai,
Daya Ganga wat,
Sateri Ganga wat,
Bawan pada vadtiyaro;
Mathon layun kat,

Ek mari santwati Ganga,
Wat deya manjaney,
Lavadiya Tari teg,
Zadach nadi khav aaton,
Ajmero khamb aanto,
Malot Hoye ghayare ghato,
Bhaghye-ro nadya-nalo hoto ghato,
Chet waira nada,
Chavad hāt jagā koodgore |8|

Dhadi to vasya gaon,
Bhar rupiyari pasi,
Teg maro Raghuro Vaghya,
Chari pada khasi,
Raghuro Wagha, Ver machayo Bavan Kaltire |9|

Meaning: I pray Sadguru and Goddess Sharda, Saraswati. May Saraswati sit in my throat and help me in singing this song from the bottom of my heart.

Seva Naik from Lavadiya clan was moving with his *Tanda* and reached the mountains near Sirpur, and Deogad forts.

The Deoraja of Deogad called Seva to his court. The Gavari Komti of Narsapet told him in the court to admit in writing that they (the Gavari Komti) are Chauvans and are invincible.

Seva Naik told, that the Komti was from a 'Jangad' or 'Ghetla' clan while he (Seva) was from Rajput geneology, from a brave stalk. As such this was an insult to him (Seva) as he was from the race of Raghu. He would not be carried away by bluffs, but kill them.

Then a battle ensued in which the Udavats, Chandavats, Vadtiyas etc. used their swords, javellins, shields etc. and a horrible darkness followed. Hit by a bullet (?), Seva's head fell in the Hariya garden.

There was none who could fight with Seva Naik. He was born in Raghu geneology. He did not retreat and this Seva from lavadiya clan showed bravery.

Wagh came to know of Seva's death. He was annoyed and attacked the enemy. The war drums started beating at this sign. Wagh from Raghu geneology called his warriors who were brave like lions. All Samants were asked to give-up their work and join.

This army crossed all rivers etc. though they were in spate and reached Narsipet. He destroyed the mountain fort and cut the heads of enemy and seized the enemy. He taught a lesson to the enemy and avenged the death of his brother.

When Wagha and his brave army was proceeding for this battle, Mahanadi and other rivers/nullas were in spate. All of them prayed the river, "Oh, Gangamata, give us a path to go, after war we shall offer you the heads of enemy as flowers. Give us the strength to cross rivers". Thus they crossed the rivers, jumping over 14 hands breadth (about 21 feet) of the rivers.

Vasha, a Dhadi Banjara has sung this Povada (song). Give him handful of rupees, give again and again. The Wagha from Raghu clan had shown great bravery, his fame being spread in all four directions and he took vengence on enemy.

This heroic song tells about the ethnic roots of the Banjara carrying them back to Mewad and linking with the Rajputs and the great Raghu-vancha and as such apart from being a historical depiction, it also links the Banjara to a settled people from whom they travelled away. The worship of Siva *bhaya* (or seva bhaiya) and reminding the community of his great deeds is the immediate purpose of the song.

However, Povada as a performing art is typical to Maharashtra in general and Western Maharashtra in particular in which heroic deeds of the Maratha warriors (who also claim a distant linkage with the Rajputs) are described. Hence, the poetic form also shows an impact of Maharashtra where the Banjaras have settled of late.

Another song is praise of the great Seva Bhaya is given below:

Dali Roraya / Chauryaynsh kotro, seva Rajiya,
At madech dera dada, atmodech kot,
Vasyajeere melmai / seva kargo chot,
Kaik lute juar, bajri, Kaik lute raji,
Vasyajire melmai / seva lute Bani |1|

Dali roraya Chauraynshi kot,
Sevar abran hoti, jabran hoti,
Jabran hoti koi,
Ek seva na hote,
To Sabki sunnat hoti,
Dali roraya / Chauryanshi kot,
Seva Raji Thor |2|

Oh residents of Delhi, Seva became king of eighty four (Chauryanshi, in Marathi, this is 84 in figures) forts. The tents and camps of the Badshah's (Mughal kings) were as invincible as forts, even then Seva entered them and deceived the Badshah's men. A lot of Jowar, bajra and ragi were looted. Seva put his life in danger. Those eighty-four forts were beyond description. But for Seva, all of us would have been subjected to *Sunta* i.e. converted to Muhammadanism.

Lakhu Banjara

This song shows the qualities of Banjara in Hindi words:

Sab thāt pada rah javega,
Jab lad chalega banjara,
Tu hai Lakkhi banjara,
Tanda tera bhari hai,
Gophal dilme mat rahana tu,
Bahot bada beopari hai |1|

Namakka, misri, kandgiri,
Phauhi saman rakhata hai,
Ganim tuze ghabarata hai |2|

Beopar tera sachcha hai,
Aor khudaka tu hai pyara,
Lakha ashrafi, lakkhi tole,
Kon karega bevhara |3|

Nur gajarka tane lagi,
Vemne kaptase mara gaya,
Vo nayak tha merahi dhani |4|

Jab aankajāki chot padi,
Roneka macha hari gul sara,
Samsher bhaloka mara |5|

The Banjara marches with his goods leaving his belongings. The Tanda of Lakhu Banjara is great and he should always be alert, being a big trader. The song continues praising the bravery of Banjara community.

Changes Due to English Rrule

Jan vegi bhikar,
aba kai chalniya far. |1|
Jepar Jor kar Sarkar,
lacta laptato valik khave
Khoto karad darbar. |2|
Dhartir upar raj kare,
Pherangi Badshaha,
Angrejari tek sakal chha,
Kaka badi malakhepar. |3|
Paro badlayo, sure mardesh

My country has changed completely, people have become bankrupt. Now people are helpless.

The pleaders take money and twist simple and straight matters, and present false thing in courts.

Under English rule, our peoples' condition has worsened. Every thing has changed in our country.

This song is an appeal to the Gor-Banjara for remembering the deeds of their leader, and is of modern origin.

Naikero phiteni upkar re, mar gor bhai,
redo dhagane bhai nayaka nayaki dego nir,
ladeni lader veto vevar, koni vetete mar
gorur vavar,
Bhadekariri mal bhar mare gaurero juno
salanger,
Kori koreti lagto to dar, remar gor bhai. |1|
Gor bandhan chhida chhidar, reshamero
ghagaro sadkeri dor,
Bandi barkashi bar bar dor, hatem
ladki disram sur,
Jana nayak lido avator re. |2|
Kul kayado nayak liyayo, mar gorun sukhi
banayo
Gamo gan dharam bandhayo, jod dhanda
karo sen jatayo
des kesula nai morare mar gor bhai. |3|
Lakhanem husar vir mar gor,
pageti pag aanga badha gor,
lat padi vot Englis bat kar, pankha
lagan dada bethorer ghar,

aab boleni nayake sawai re mar gor bhai. |4|

Kavi Tukaram garo bhajan nayakere
nameti aapano vajan,
Vor kan koni veto dushmen, sajan
sen len chalo bhai saman,
vose aiketi chalo kego
sen re mar gor bhai. |5|

Naik has obliged us and has paid attention to out Gor (Banjara) brothers and we shall never be able to compensate his obligations.

(1) They (The Banjara) had no farms or land and used to carry goods on payment as carriers. This was their trade and they used a different dress. They were afraid of people from other communities.

(2) Other communities used to look down upon the Banjara who used to wear silken *Ghagra* (long petticoats) and long shirts with twelve chords. With a stick in hand and sporting of long mustaches made the Banjara look brave. It was during those days that (Vasantrao) Naik was born.

(3) Naik brought Tenancy Act and made the Gor Banjara happy. Irrigation facilities and dams were built in many towns and cottage industries were provided to people. Due to Naik, the Banjaras area has flowered like a Palas tree.

(4) My Gor-Banjara brothers are intelligent and are acquiring education. They speak English fluently. There are electric fans in their houses i.e. they are happy and now the people from other communities call them as Naiks.

(5) The poet from pandhurna of name Tukaram says that the Banjaras got status and prestige due to Naik. Naik had no enemies, and he had kept contacts with all good and polite people, similarly, all Gor-Banjaras also should imitate him.

This is a typical song indicating the social change in the Banjaras of Vidarbha and the role of Naik family of Pusad in general and Shri Vasantrao Naik (Ex-Chief Minister or Maharashtra who was from the Banjara) in particular. His deeds and example are placed before the community through this song. The poet is one Tukaram from Pandhurna.

Moth yadi dhavalem bolire nayaka,
suni padi haveli
patlya pandewar aate the, ghar ghar
hajeri lete the,
Aik neta na reta to, gormati jangadya,
kera te te,
Uto samajen kargo sauli re nayaka
panadada dorkin peratoro phetya,
Kori kor keteta aayo,
Gormatya, nankya, nankya kundi kunda,
marrete bhata,
budha budha korikar kartete thata,
kun kai tu phernako killi re nayaka,
lagamele mala doldar shobha,
phekre chhodaka khare gobha gobha,
Khete mai biyan bai, lai daba,
nanakyase chhoran koi kere balu,
Koi kere baba,
Kali yadi nagenai duliri nayaka.

After the death of Vasantrao Naik his wife feels lonely in the big house. But for him the Gor-Banjaras would have been treated as *Jangad* i.e. outsiders and of lower status.

The old dress in the days of grand-mother and father, which was criticised has been changed due to the influence of Naik.

During Naik's regime, the land became horticultural and several fruits started growing in it. The Banjaras progressed and their children are now called by names like Balu, Baba* etc. The crops on black soil are now standing and rocking like snakes.

This song depicts how the Banjara community progressed and acquired status among the non-Banjara people in Vidarbha Maharashtra due to the leadership of Shri Vasantrao Naik.

Jitu Maro Raj

Aang- aang ghodlo bhiduye naval bani,
Joi ton jitu maro raj.
Pacha baniro ratha chale bani,

---

* *Balu, Baba*, are terms used to call children in the rural/urban areas, in families who enjoy good status.

Toi ton jitu maro raj.
Pan bida chabuye naval bani,
Joi ton jitu mari raj,
chokhese raluye naval bani,
joi ton jitu maro raj.

If brave people come together and fight shoulder to shoulder, our regime can be saved.

A chariot can work if all wheels and horses come together, this can keep our regime safe.

If betel leaves are eaten as a pan (together) the work is done.

If the king is good the regime is saved.

Gol

Pan panchait raja Bhojer cha bha,
Bhain sak pancha re jag yekti yek sawai,
Gadre parra kangla hathi pareri dhal,
Ye sagaro kai parkya, parkya Hira mairo lal,
Hira Hira kya kahe, Hira pado bazar me,
Khakri le laptaya, aasolri padi bund
pot nibji bhaji
Sagali saga malgi to, sital vegi chhati,
Dholo ghoto hasalo khuti talo lagam
Aamryai kacheri umryar beska,
Ye sagaro kai valkya, valkha bira majro lal,
Hira hira kya kape, Hira pade bazar me.
khakri le laptaya,
lakparvana kasturi bhejiv, kholuto parmal mare,
Joluto purich puri,
Jater beti bhukiyaro, beta nato buvo yen
sari Jag dise,
Jasao gol mito, voso saga mito aachaki bat.

The song describes the panchayat of Raja Bhoj in which each panch was wiser than his pancha brothers. It describes how a case of a diamond was settled.

A Tale of Creation

This world was created from *Jambav* who gave birth to Hepumuni and Raktamuni (Shiva). First a beautiful Goddess was created who gave birth to a child. This child was created in the same manner in which Lord Ganesh was created by Parvati from the soil film on body skin. This child gave birth to the population. The first men included Kachchap (kashyap), Dhaj (Dhwaj), Kandhaj (Kushdhwaj), Karan (Karna) Thida, Shada, Nathad, Jodhan, Khimad, Mota, Mola, etc. Mola is also supposed to be Lord Shrikrishna's friend.

The Bhukiya'a War Against Vadatiya

Bhimsingh was a well known Banjara warrior. During his regime there was a war between the Bhukiyas and the Vadatiyas. The Bhukiyas were victorious, but the Vadatiyas mixed poison in the drinking water lake of the Bhukiyas and killed many of them and then cut heads of many Bhukiyas also. Since then, the Bhukiyas tell the Vadatiyas that their faces look like girls and there is a blot on their faces. They shall take revenge.

The Vadatiyas give a reply saying that the blot on their faces is nothing as compared to the Bhukiyas. Bhukiya forefather was born in *Malya* caste and his father and mother were not known. He was brought-up by a Brahmin when he ruined. Hence their class had a big blot.

The Four Yugas

One Dhadi Jayatram has written a song on Lumba Naik. He tells us that Jagdeo Pawar cut his head and offered it to Jagdamba in the *Satya-yuga*. In the *Treta-yuga*, Lakha Phulani offered his queen by name Naranga to uphold religion. He than tells us that in the *Dwapar yuga* a king by name Vakado gave his son Tarachand for religious purpose and in *Kali-yuga*, Lumba Naik spread his fame in four countries. He gave birth to four sons viz. Chintaman, Tarachand, Deoji and Bhiluchari and then died. This looks like a mythical version of the Banjara History.

APPENDIX-I

SOME MORE SONGS IN BANJARI DIALECT

THE BANJARA folk songs depict a strong orientation towards the Bhakti-cult and abound in profuse reference to Hindu Gods and Goddesses as well as Avatars and the Saints including those saints who are from the *Varkari Sampradaya* i.e. the worshippers of Lord Vitthal (incarnation of Lord Vishnu) at Pandharpur.

However, the above references though picked-up due to years and decades of settled life in Vidarbha (Maharashtra) are a part of their traditional worship of Lord Rama and Shrikrishna brought by them right from the days of emigration from Mewad/Marwar in Rajasthan. But the poet by name Tukaram (not the Saint Tukaram, but a modern poet by that name) claiming his residence at Pandharuna, has composed many songs which are spiritual and give references of almost all Gods, Goddesses, Avatars, Saints from religious mythology, epics, to the Saints in Maharashtra. He even refers to national leaders, freedom fighters like Bhagat Singh to Mahatma Gandhi and Banjara leaders like late Shri Vasantrao Naik from Pusad (District Yeotmal) who was Chief Minister of Maharashtra for many years and worked for the socio-economic upliftment and education of the Banjaras in Maharashtra. Thus, his songs or Bhajans are modern in origin and reflect the changing social structure of the community and their attitudes. He has composed songs on the harmful effects of liquor, Bhang, Ganja etc. and urges their people to lead a simple, honest life *sans* all addictions and excesses. Though his songs may not be termed as folk-songs in a strict sense (as they are not of community origin and oral transmission) their relevance and importance for the Banjara, their being composed in the Banjari language and the fact that they are composed by an illiterate person for their community deserve their mention. A few songs (in which his name appears) are given earlier, but the other songs are reproduced in this appendix so as to acquaint readers with their style, scope and content.

Bhajan

(A Pooja Song by Tukaram)

Gangau Gauvari maro tukari aajore
Kavi Tukaro vajo nangararo vaja re,
Hat khanjeri naubat ghori sanal maro aawajre,
Chavlen ukali bitali, bhuva kidor fuleri kamoli,
Ore saru ton m aat balau,
Sir-kamleri phool chadhau,
Paach tatweri batti lagau,
Jon satraviri pali parad,
Char vederi chari hatem,
Sahi shastrero bhala lagan
Manebhaveti Puja banauchu aajo re,
Kavi Juka adnyani anphad, Budhi yen kahi kaleni,
Guru Budhiti lakharo, lakhere aajo re,

Gana — Gau Gauri Goddess. He describes her as holding four *vedas* in four hands a javellin of six *Sastras* in her hand and offers his head like a lotus and the sandalwood in the form of five elements (Panch-Tatva). He concludes by saying that an illiterate like him is performing her worship.

Bandi gamano niti kamano, chauranshise phero chha,
Aayo pamno didan, ekadam pali chukanichh,
Aang vadho thano, puchchiye keno lebu jabani deno chcha,
Ram nameri bhari hatdi, Bhav bhaktiri bandh gathidi,
Aacho. -aacho wan leno, mat bandha grabo,
Didan bharal sukhere sal, abhimanen margo u Shishupal
Sagarem Jano shikhal pohno,
Sangat karo aacheri badhatiro man,
Dhokem ghaldiy dushaman,
Lan sane kan besno, aachi wat shikno
Ekalo kag kido naikan ron malgo man,
Jaso Harichand sapnem de dino dan,
Aachen var khechano balan par kochano,

Kavi Tukari padi lalkar, aajar tem
Mal koni sawar,
Harinam bhajano santem ramno.

Man passes through a vicious circle of eighty four lakhs births. To overcome these successfully he advises to follow the path of truth and morality. Pray Ram and have faith. Keep good company as enemies way-lay you from good path.

Lankaro Raja (Bhajan)

Lankaro raja lakhopati, Vu abhimanen
nachagore,
Dharma bholo ramtim, betho fasar davem
phasagor,
Valya koli pap kargo, Ramer nameti targor,
Harichand rajar sapner katha,
Kashin lego shravan mata-n-pita,
Dasharatha ban maro, dharnin padtani
margor,
Jarasandhen Bhim chiran feko,
Nal rajamayi motho liyayo Voko,
Sudamer bodhe pova khalen priya bangor,
Ravanaro Hanuman balgo madi,
Draupadir Dushasan khechagor sadi,
Hirnyakasuper Bhagatsing chhati chirgor,
Lachmanen lago saktir ban,
Hanuman layo paden vatan,
Parlad marokoni telem talatani bachanor
Mahadev Bhashyan dino var lago ghor,
Hanuman Ramen dekho saru chhatin chir,
Tuka vacho puran, puranem she van Kalgor.

Raja of Lanka (Ravana) become proud and adamant but was ruined, Dharmaraj lost due to gambling Valya Koli committed sins, but all these could get salvation due to Ram-nam.

The poet then lists and reminds the listeners the following episodes from puran viz. Raja Harischandra, Shravan — Bal, Raja Dashrath, Jarasandha-Bhim feud, Raja Nal, the Krishna-Sudama friendship, Draupadi-Vastraharan, Hiranya Kashyapu, Veer Bhagatsingh, the power that hit Laxmana (in Ramayana), Prahlad

Bal, Bhasmasur, and narrates the morals from these stories.

Poet Tukaram tries to combine mythical and historical episodes and stories for placing before the Banjara, high morals and philosophical message.

Vasneti Javal Chalo (Bhajan)

Kido mehnat jiva lai laire,
Vesneti jival chalo,
Vair n malo, daruto mati kukadi nai kaj
Piletani daru damo gada nai maj jaso aavago,
Van Ravanaro raj parbhati bolnuto chhut von laj,
Sari supharin gal por teje maire,
Lagagi bimari jana sarirat khastakteti khas,
Jana laren wal wal natya potya samlan,
Godgad has dadi deri gali taro vejay satyanas.
Phido Jindgir rakha ejjat ghoture,
Daneti ghalro regharagha Jav aakhimai gid nakem ritha,
Aao Koi bol janaop vichakan Jav lagago Kathen,
Tari eka pav chal go Jaro ivan garane mair,
Ghan veti umar pan barch vegi kat aang moksha pade na,
Jayen malri koni vat yersaru bhiya vagnu kar
Nit aache aache van lek di daner hat jaktero,
Nam lel kamati chheir,
palapi Hari namero aaki kar lal,
bhajan kar bhagwaner,
Zakmariya kal santen savad lago Vitthal
Namero, petrolbhar gadich veyeni fel,
Tuka divano vego bhajnere maire,

Even if you exert hard, if you are an addict, you cannot prosper.

After drinking wine you become as uncontrollable as king Ravana and lose your honour and became shameless.

Diseases befall upon you and you lose your bodily strength, the life is ruined and people laugh at you.

Money is lost, life is shortened, so behave properly don't lose days of life in addition.

If you want to follow the path of *Moksha* (Salvation) take the name of God for which nothing is to be spent i.e. does not cost you any thing.

Utter the name of Hari and do Bhajan of God which was done by

Saints who worshipped Lord Vitthal. Put the Petrol of Ram-Nam in your Vehicle (*Gadi* - i.e. earthly life) so that it won't fail in the way and reach you to salvation.

Aika Kareri Zanj

Aika kareri Zanj vaj chun chun chun,
Pane thali vaj chhun chhun chhun,
Motivalaro Bhimaro chhora aai valo re,
Bana nako sira thoru vala re, taro bhayro,
ghoro nangara,
Gyar parser Umar kholam chhodlego dhor,
Sakha bhima thore lar ghunghadi lidi khandepar
aang aang,
Basari ghararo lar lar dhor. |1|
Sarsi kotharo khola dhan karo kero gola bhima
nayakero bala,
Vere kan ghani kala Jagadambari sajan gayo
gojanako khola. |2|
Bhata rada layo het tholiti maro onp chot,
Paner tod layo deth, Zanje kardino fit bhajan
bolto,
Bhuk lagi dukh lago pet. |3|
Dhud layo seva hira paninak ghotelago
gar sakan,
Karo lego shira deveri aardas kara pantu
kero yen bhut,
Lago diwand vego hira. |4|
Saka chatan dekho sari munda mitho vego
bhay sat vatago,
Var nam amar rego pandumaro Tuka
Kero sen dego degi. |5|

Tandero Panch Nekiro

Tandero panch nekiro manch udar manero
chay ho mitha bole,
Valo dhakto chale valo aaso pudhari koni chaya ma,
Kerchu ma kai jalan kero Kai kboni bhita,
Koni yen chhodo ho, sukhi vavdim janrat pado,
Ekmekeri sale tandem kal khichadi kervalo

Keni chay viye.
Badnam karo aachocho kam gokulvasti chay ho
ma khoto,
Kerochu kai koni bhiya koni tin bar. |1|
Bolen bolko kamen halko kam katalo koni chay,
Maryadeti Ranu sarmeti mamu gunvan
bai chay ho. |2|
Dikhayan dholo khetiro katalo kam katalya koni chay,
Shai mankyam besha, gadgad hasya khulchati
Koni chay ho. |3|
Viksan chale palo kashta kare valo gunman
Shetkari chay ho,
Dāru pidadya gappajhodya aaso pudhari
koni chay. |4|
Kukadiro gunda ida nisar banda, duglya
Mankya koni chay,
Sadaro tanda samajem zenda deshbhakta chay ho. |5|
Kero Tukaram karo aacho kam, Ramram
bhajo Om aacho,
Riy eka mekero sanman sendo manpan jet jakon
Bharmeti rei chay. |6|

This *Bhajan* tells how the *Panchas* in *Tanda*, the leaders, and others in the village should behave so that they will earn name and reputation. Importance of unity and of absence of addiction to liquor etc. is stressed.

Tarl Kotiti

Tari koti ti, talo khagochi, talo mat khore
mar nayak
Bapu re keni man, lovdiri aasha, kudodi aau tare.
Marvadem jivda maro zurchanir,
Samki yadi rire jari tangdi rov mothi yadi kashi,
Layo kukai kargo prabhu tadakodi dalhal roy moth
yadi nir. |1|
Viramare reto, pamani lato, lovadi daroto, dino
koni vira dev man nir. |2|
Samki yadi rire aavgi tangdi dai sali aatni,
Ghunghato vghadi, rangeti kal bhur chhori nir. |3|
Chand sarikhi surat jetari aaj kono mali bodi,

Kal bhur chhori vat bai pori nir. |4|
Sasubai ronre, taras bhari, yen dabau keri
dusar bodi,
Lau Jeta laleri, rat-dan kam karari nir. |5|
Kavi Tukaram Garo bhajan, daneti dan jare
vatan bāp
Aayo pamni leyer nir. |6|

This song praises Sumki-Yadi i.e. Goddess Samki Mātā and her influence on domestic life.

Baap Aay Yadin

Baap aayo yadin pamani leye vasure,
deklidi bapen
Yadi vege khushre, Ore sasuro ken ghano
taraser.
Hate mai lakdi laghabhagh aaye re yadi
nakri gobar,
Von dekha pachayer samaki vor galo pakdon
dalhal royo ran. |1|
Susubai vori datalan aaire kamdhando
chhodden barkari,
Tuire ghor lago sukaricha lakdire nair. |2|
Tukan pucharich samdan bai re kamdhandero
dan kimchalo,
Aayore pamni lejau mari samki bai re. |3|
sat din daneri karar bandh dini sasubai re,
Dhokdev sasun bai chali aayire sobatnero
galo pakdan roi re. |4|
Char panch dan sukheti khadivoi re, saṃki keri,
Bapen man meli tui re, sat danero karar bandhi,
Panch danem hoto aaye re. |5|
Kavi Tukaram garo bhajane mai re,
Samki sariki,
Yadi bai bano koi re, gunen man mal santeri
Gavai re. |6|

A Bhajan song is praise of Samki Mata which gives instance from family life.

Desh Maro Bada Rangelo

Dhakda fuleti lal chcha, pan desh maro bado
rangilo chha
Jime timen kal ghusaro chcha,
Karmele kamai jen khecharocha,
E aadar kodiyaro malo chcha. |1|
Zad chodhan heteti dekhore chcha,
Janjoli ven vode kan,
Chutre chha, gad jitre petem kalo chcha. |2|
De palya mankyaro jamrocha,
Mitho boltani matalab lutarocha,
Bachatani chalo motho hanglocha. |3|
Tuka kero jaso balad charrocha,
Lalachi labad bhako marrocha,
Futo thutar munden kalo chcha. |4|

This song criticises those who talk sweet words but do harmful things. Such persons are dangerous for the country. The poet asks to liquidate such black faces.

Desh Bhagatero Itihas

Desh bhagatero itihas aakin kholo premeti bolo,
Deshesaru pran dege jive pe Udar. Osi boli bolo ho
Bolo bolo.
Bolo ho javnero karlo bhalor,
Jijayadire Udari aayo dese saru deh Zijayo,
Chatrapati Shivaji huyo, dese sare jiv bitayo,
Mat vago sotare hitevas. |1|
Mardani vo Zansiwali bal putepar band meli,
Kaik chhodke madi haveli varichhode koni santeri boli,
Vosi firti karo hamkhas. |2|
Mahatma Gandhi ra padi pukar jivepari ya vegi udor,
Maharana Pratap viz Bhagatsinha ranlih,
Yenduncha kar veti khas. |3|
Bhimro vu Sevalal, purthiro vu vegu mol,
Santeri Zendi hatem len, nito ghanem Nikliya tel,
Hanu Tukari margo sevalal. |4|
Pandit Nehru, Jagrore matlabe saru,
Jivan aayeni var varu, Vasantraveri
Lalkar maru,
Garo bhajan Pandurnaro Tuke sero das. |5|

Satyanshiro Saal Aayo

(The Draught of 1987)

Satyanshiro sal aayo, khan, khan, khan, khan,
Vege bhan bhan bhan bhan, maro bhiyare.
Khisa vege thale,
Maro mamare Jangyo vege thile, maro
Kakare aab bharnem bharnem chale re.

Per mele mung, barbati seri vakad naki,
Cheoti, savisarpya kilo boti,
dukrip veshi ghani dati, chit melo to
madi bandhau,
Ghani chyat beti. |1|

Vakde vadad pere karadi seri vakdanaki khildi,
Nikli Koni khagi sheldi, mati kharo lago maldi,
Roj kharoto phadi sapari, mlari
Koni baldi. |2|

Megharaj dino tadi, seri vala nako godi,
Chhori valayeri padi,
Hundari chal ghani badi, khaldi baldi
vavram dekhanu,
Kati chheni medi matilar lago vedo
Jat vat bhanbhan vegi,
Todo khodi chheni phiko pado mundo,
Marchya chheni roro kundo,
Aapkal Holin Koi reyeni, Kul kadhiy dando. |3|

Karjaro vego ghano laphada, vajago shero
Phuto daphada,
Ruyen dekha bete jabhada, Aapkan peren
maleni kapada, Jangya phatro thigli lagaro
kayi kariye-Bapda. |4|

Pandhurnaro kavi kero Tuka, devshen kar nako tika
Aattechareri vego hak, garani kate talu lakha,
Vasant kaka sen jatago, Jod dhanda kheti pika. |5|

This song describes conditions during the draught of 1987.

CLAN NAMES

Aadot
Aamgot
Aanawat
Aarond
Aayyot
Ajmera
Badhawat
Balawat
Bandawat
Bandhawat
Banot
Barmawat
Bhanchawat
Bhangawat
Bhartawat
Bhegawat
Bhojawat
Bhukiya
Bochadot
Bonda
Buchawat
Chajawat
Chandawat
Chandot
Chaundawat
Chauvan
Chayyot
Chinawat
Chitawat
Dahawat
Dalwan
Dedawat
Delawat
Depawat
Deplan
Devawat
Dhanawat
Dharawat
Dhasadi
Dhasawat
Dhirawat
Dudhawat
Dulawat
Dumawat
Dungarot
Fulaya
Galawat
Gangawat
Gaur
Ghandawat
Gidawat
Gorham
Hadawat
Hajawat
Hapawat
Hardev
Hasawat
Jadawat
Jagwat
Jamanawat
Jatot
Jesawat
Jetsalot
Jinawalo
Jodhawali
Jodhawat
Jongawat
Kadawat
Kalawat
Kamawat
Kanhawat
Kanthwala
Kardawat
Karha
Karnawat
Kasanawat
Keluta
Khamawat
Khanawat
Khetawat
Khola
Kitawat
Kotawali
Kukarichya
Kunpawat
Kunthawat
Kurawat
Lagawat
Lakhawat
Lakshot
Lala
Lalawat
Lavdiya
Lotawat
Lumbawat
Lunsawat
Madrichya
Malwat
Malwat
Mangawat
Meghawat
Menawat
Mertiya
Mokawat
Molan
Mood
Motawat
Motiwalo
Muchal
Mulawat
Munawat
Mundawat
Nagawat
Nalawat
Nenawat
Padiya
Palosiya
Paltiya
Paltiya
Panchanawat
Panchwat
Pangot
Patarwal
Pemani
Pepawat
Perajat
Phulawat
Pipawat
Povawat
Punawat
Rajawat
Rammiya
Ranawal
Ranawat
Ratla
Rupawat
Sadarat
Sadarat
Sadawat
Sakra
Saktawat
Salawat
Sandol
Sangawat

Sewawat	Tarwani	Udhawat	Wangot
Siraya	Tejawat	Vadatiya	Wani
Somawat	Thakran	Vijarawat	Wankdot
Tainsond	Tunwar	Vinjarawat	Wojgar
Tarawat	Udawat	Vislawat	Zarpala

APPENDIX-III

WORDS SHOWING RELATIONSHIP

Bahanoi – Sister's husband
Bahen – Sister
Bahu – Daughter-in-Law
Buaaji – Father's sister's husband
Buaa – Father's sister
Devarani – Husband's younger brother's wife
Devar – Husband's younger brother
Jamai – Son-in-Law
Jethani – Husband's elder brother's wife
Jeth – Husband's elder brother
Mausaji – Mother's sister's husband
Mausi – Mother's sister
Nanandoi – Husband's sister's husband
Nanand – Husband's sister
Sali – Wife's younger sister

NAMES OF PLANTS/TREES

		Botanical Names
Ber	–	(Ziziphus jujuba) (Indian Jujub)
Bhang Charas Ganja	–	Cannabis Sativa syn. Cannabis indica.
Ganeri	–	Cochlospermum gossynium.
Ghaneri	–	Lantana indica
Jamun	–	Eugenia Jambolana
Khair (Katechu)	–	Acacia catechu
Mahua	–	Madhuca indica (Bessia latifolia)
Margosa	–	Azadirachta indica (Neem) (Melia azadirachrta)
Mehendi	–	Lawsonia inermis (Henna)
Palas	–	Butea frendosa (Fire of the Forest)
Rui	–	Calotropis procera (Mader /Aak)
Salai	–	(Boswellia serrata)
Teer	–	Cajanus cajan (Pigeon Pea)
Tilli	–	Sesamum indicum (Sesame)
Umbar	–	Ficus glomerata

BIBLIOGRAPHY

Karve, Irawati, 1962: *Marathi Lokanchi Sanskruthi*, Deshmukh and Co., Pune.

Nanjudayya, Iyyer and K. Anantha Krishnan, 1928: *The Mysore Tribes and Castes*, Vol. I, Mysore.

Patil, Baliram Hiraman, 1936: *Gor Banjara Lokancha Itihas Baliram Patil Smarak Samiti*, Yeotmal.

Russell, R.V. and Hiralal, 1975: *Tribes and Castes of the Central Provinces of India*, Vol. II, Cosmo Publications, (Ist .Ed. 1916) Reprint, Delhi.

INDEX